CHASING THE PANDA

How an UNLIKELY PAIR

of ADVENTURERS

WON the RACE to CAPTURE

the MYTHICAL "WHITE BEAR"

For Quentin

CHASING THE PANDA

How an UNLIKELY PAIR

of ADVENTURERS

WON *the* RACE *to* CAPTURE

the MYTHICAL "WHITE BEAR"

by Michael Kiefer

FOUR WALLS EIGHT WINDOWS NEW YORK

PUBLISHED BY
Four Walls Eight Windows
39 West 14th Street, room 503
New York, N.Y., 10011

Visit our website at http://www.4w8w.com

First printing April 2002.

Library of Congress Cataloging-in-Publication data on file.

ISBN 1-56858-223-4

10   9   8   7   6   5   4   3   2   1

Printed in Canada
Book design by Sara E. Stemen
Panda frontispiece by Hank Tusinski

CONTENTS

CHASING THE PANDA

How an UNLIKELY PAIR

of ADVENTURERS

WON *the* RACE *to* CAPTURE

the MYTHICAL "WHITE BEAR"

The trek to the Sichuan-Tibet borderlands was like travelling into a classical Chinese watercolor painting, a journey in time as well as in space. Courtesy Mrs. Vivian Dai.

CHAPTER ONE

THE PANDA FIRST

He heard shots, and the Lolo hunters were shouting *beixiong,* "white bear," which is what they called the giant panda in that time and place. Quentin Young started to run, as best he could, uphill through a landscape that could have been a classical Chinese painting, full of snow and mists and mountains and bamboo thickets. He was gasping for breath in the thin air at 12,000 feet, cursing to himself, perhaps cursing aloud. The hunters had been ordered not to shoot, because he wanted to capture the giant panda alive.

The American woman was foundering in the snow somewhere below him, forever slipping, caught on thorns, and he worried that if he charged ahead to reprimand the hunters, to even see what they were shooting at, he'd lose her in the forest. As troublesome as she was, he was responsible for her. She'd refused to stay in camp, and she *was* the boss, so he had to give in to her insistence.

It was 1936, November 19, somewhere in the mountains on the Sichuan-Tibetan border, 1,900 miles from Shanghai, where they'd started their journey nearly two months before. Young was 22, a Westernized Chinese who was trying to make a name for himself as a naturalist. He was tall and dark, with movie-star good looks and a stylish black pompadour. The woman was Ruth Harkness, darkly attractive despite her unusual features, with long black hair that she wrapped around her head and covered with a turban. She was 35, a New York dress designer, and recently widowed. Her late husband, William Harvest Harkness, Jr., had been a bring-'em-back-alive hunter who'd traveled to the Dutch East Indies to capture Komodo lizards, which he brought to the Bronx Zoo. But that accomplishment did not stop the zoological establishment from chuckling at his boasts that he'd bring eight or ten or more giant pandas back from China.

By today's standards, this seems no great feat. In 1936 it was unprecedented. Giant pandas lived several days' trek even from remote villages like Zhaopo, which was a weeks-long voyage from civilized Shanghai. Few had even been seen alive by Westerners and then only through the cross hairs of rifles. When one was shot by the sons of President Theodore Roosevelt in 1929, it was as if they had hunted down a unicorn. Everyone mistakenly thought they were the first "Occidentals" to ever see one alive, and this was somehow a great achievement on their part. Over the next six years, rich Western hunters killed three more, and because those Great White Hunters bragged of the ferocity of the giant pandas they shot, zoologists were not even sure they could be taken alive, though more than one hunter wanted to try.

Such expeditions drew great public acclaim and the newspapers made media heroes of the adventurers who staged them. Animal study was just moving away from the extended hunting trips in which animals were killed to be mounted in museums such as the Field in Chicago, where the Roosevelts' panda is still displayed. The new trend was to capture the animals alive, to bring them triumphantly back to civilization and put them on display in zoos.

Bill Harkness's panda-hunting mission had been much ballyhooed in the press, but he hardly made it out of Shanghai. He couldn't get the proper government permits. Then he took ill with throat cancer, which spread to his stomach and killed him.

Ruth Harkness wandered to China to tidy up his estate. She was not the kind of person to let better judgment get in the way of her decisions. So, on a whim, she decided to take over her husband's ill-fated expedition. She fired his partner, an American expatriate named Floyd Tangier Smith, and met with Quentin Young's older brother Jack, a well-respected naturalist who had traveled with the Roosevelts. Jack Young recommended that she talk to Quentin, whom he had trained. Together the brothers had hunted takin (a horned animal peculiar to the highlands of central Asia that combines features of the ox, goat and antelope) and golden monkeys and rare pheasants for American museums and zoos and private collectors, alternately battling bandits and entertaining the warlords that controlled the primitive rural areas.

Of course, if it was already laughable that a man named Harkness thought he'd capture pandas, it was downright ludicrous to the zoological establishment that a woman could, especially given her choice for expedition leader, a 22-year-old "Chinaman," with an Anglo-sounding name.

But Young managed to get Harkness up the Yangzi River to Chongqing, overland by car to Chengdu, then hired a cook and hunters and coolies for the final hundred-mile walk—having her carried or wheeled in a wheelbarrow much of the way—to the village of Zhaopo and the bamboo thickets beyond.

He had seen panda sign in the days before. The shots by the trigger-happy hunters probably meant they'd sighted one, more likely shot it to eat it, to sell the hide, and then deny they'd even seen it. Anyway, the local hunters couldn't really understand why the foreigners were so obsessed with the white bear. Its meat was rubbery, its hide coarse, though some villagers thought that sleeping on a panda skin would bring good luck.

And though the Roosevelts and other hunters had told their tales of how fierce the giant panda was, the villagers knew that if one wandered into camp looking for handouts, they could bang pots to shoo it away.

Nonetheless, as long as this foreigner, Harkness, was willing to pay them by the day, they could make panda hunting last as many days as possible. "You can always fool a foreigner," went the local wisdom.

This hotheaded young Chinese, however, was a puzzlement to the locals. He spoke the language of the foreign devil, but spoke their own language as well. He ate the peculiar foods that she ate—or salt fish and tofu just as they did, too. His name, even, "Yang," in Chinese with one inflection meant "over the seas, foreigner." They were willing to fool him anyway.

For his part, Young had little faith in his employees to do anything more than take money day to day, lead him aimlessly through the forest and lie to him about how difficult it was to find pandas. His temper was heating up as he waited for Harkness to claw her way uphill. Then he heard a baby's whimper. It was coming from the upside-down-V-shaped opening in a hollow tree, a baby panda, so young its eyes were not yet open.

4

Young wanted to put it back in the tree, assuming it would die without its mother—which he surmised the hunters had already shot. He wanted an adult bear; he'd brought chains and shackles and giant cages to restrain it.

Harkness stumbled into the clearing just as Young was pulling the cub out of its den, and she took it from his arms and cradled it like a baby. She'd brought a piece of equipment in her pack that Young had not anticipated: a baby bottle. In her mind, this baby was as good, if not better, than an adult panda. Young put the tiny animal inside his shirt and then slid back downhill to camp over the snow on the seat of his pants.

As Young stayed in the forest to hunt for more pandas, Harkness trekked back to Shanghai and virtually smuggled her baby panda onto a ship bound for San Francisco. She named the animal after Young's sister-in-law, Su Lin, which means "a little bit of something very cute."

Harkness kept the tiny animal in her New York hotel room as she haggled with zoos over which would buy it from her. Though the New York press assumed it would end up at the Bronx Zoo, that institution's keepers feared the animal was unhealthy and passed it by. Eventually Su Lin ended up at the Brookfield Zoo in Chicago.

Even today, pandas are major zoo attractions, guaranteed revenue sources, worth fighting over, worth finding a congressman to grease the way past endangered species laws. They were even more so in 1936.

Su Lin was the most famous animal in the world. When the little panda took up residence at the Brookfield Zoo, the day's celebrities—John Barrymore, Helen Keller, even Al Capone—filed past its cage. Its popularity inspired the zoo to send Harkness back to Sichuan twice more to find a suitable mate. But there was no mating. Su Lin choked on a twig, then contracted pneumonia and died 16 months after coming to America. Then it was stuffed and put on display in the Field Museum like its Roosevelt predecessor.

Quentin Young, meanwhile, disappeared into World War II. He rode the Burma Road with an American documentary film crew and was imprisoned by the Japanese. Then he lived through revolution as the Dutch East Indies became Indonesia. He spied on the Indonesian dictator Sukarno on behalf of Nationalist China, he says, and nearly lost his life doing so. He escaped to Taiwan and worked as an editor, and then he followed his older brother to the United States. He retired to San Diego, where—as of this writing—he still lives with his second wife. But of anything he ever did in his long life, the panda expedition has haunted him the most.

After Ruth Harkness arrived in the United States, Bill Harkness's old partner, Floyd Tangier Smith, immediately claimed that she and Young had stolen the panda from his hunters in Zhaopo. In her 1938 book, *The Lady and the Panda*, Harkness derisively referred to Smith as "Zoology Jones." But no matter; he was one of the Great White Hunters, and his word carried weight. Publicly, the museum curators and zoologists acknowledged Harkness, but to this day, would-be historians, field biologists, and Chinese wags near the Wolong Panda study in Sichuan, still whisper slyly that Quentin Young and Ruth Harkness had cheated the zoological establishment. To this day, they have a hard time believing that a dilettante woman and a boy "Chinaman" could have beaten them to the catch.

Ruth Harkness became famous, Quentin Young did not. Nor did his brother Jack, who had as much experience as any naturalist working in China. Jack bounced from adventure to adventure, often guiding the Americans who would then bask in the limelight as daring adventurers. And even though they lived in an era when the public idolized the heroic men and women who scaled unclimbed peaks, mapped unexplored places, flew across uncharted bodies of water, and discovered unnamed species, the public imagination was perhaps not large enough to include heroes who weren't Anglo-American or European. Nonetheless, these men were the last living witnesses to a nearly forgotten age of exploration.

Quentin with a bear he'd shot. Courtesy Mrs. Vivan Dai.

CHAPTER TWO

QUENTIN

"The truth is the truth!"

During one of our first meetings, Quentin Young practically bellowed at me when I brought up the old dispute over whether he and Harkness had bought their panda from Smith's hunters. He admits they *would* have if given the chance. They wanted a panda, and buying one would have been a quick and economical option.

"If I lie what do I gain?"

I first met Young in 1988, while researching a magazine article about Ruth Harkness. Most of the published accounts I found about her questioned whether she'd really found the panda herself, but they were all written as if it were ancient history, without seeming to look for eyewitnesses to an adventure that had occurred only fifty years earlier. As I read Harkness's book, *The Lady and the Panda*, it occurred to me that Young might still be alive. He'd only been twenty-two when they'd caught their panda.

Besides, Harkness's descriptions of Young seemed to say more by the details left out than by those left in. I suspected they'd had an affair, and that seemed a delicious possibility, so I set out to look for him.

Because his father and brothers had all been born in the United States, I thought it doubtful that he would have remained in the Republic of China. Perhaps he was in Taiwan, or Hong Kong, or Hawaii, or California, and I started to inquire in those places.

At the same time, I looked up Harkness's 1947 obituary in the *New York Times*, which said that she was survived by a sister who still lived in Harkness's home town of Titusville, Pennsylvania. I called the library in Titusville and asked the librarian to read off the phone numbers of everyone in town with the same last name. On the third or fourth call, a startled man said that indeed, he was related to Harkness, though he didn't know much about her. But his Aunt Harriet, who was Harkness's sister, lived in a nearby nursing home, and he promised to ask her to call me. She did, and she had a phone number for Quentin Young in San Diego.

Young was alarmed at being found. He was living in a two-room apartment with his second wife, Swan, a cheery Indonesian woman of Chinese descent, but he had an unlisted number and took his mail at a post office box so no one would know where he lived. He was in the habit of taping his own phone calls. Because he'd been involved in espionage in Southeast Asia after World War II, he was still nervous about old enmities. Whether his concern was real or just in the nature of a spy's personality, I never really knew. But when I called, it was enough to make his blood pressure spike, and he suffered a stroke. After a few weeks, I persuaded him to meet with me and decide if he wanted to sit for interviews.

Michael Kiefer with Quentin Young in California in the late 1980s.
Courtesy Michael Kiefer

He was 74, but still strikingly handsome, with salt and pepper hair and an upright, dignified carriage that made him appear taller than he really was. His English was grammatically flawless, but with a decidedly Chinese lilt that ranged from a poetic whisper to an angry growl, depending on his mood—and his mood changed like the weather. He could laugh and joke one minute and then cloud over and explode with a flash of his youthful temper. He was patriarchal and demanding, an unabashedly "Oriental" male, despite his American heritage, and always insistent on keeping face.

He'd moved to California to be in the movies. He'd sold his life story to an American he met at a Jehovah's Witness congregation in Taiwan. A screenplay was commissioned, written and rewritten. Katherine Ross—he was told—had been considered to play the part of Ruth Harkness. A Chinese production company was lined up and the film was to be a historic international collaboration. And after a small fortune was spent, the whole project went away until 1990, when Young received a call from a Hollywood producer, delighted to tell him that the movie was on track again.

Young was bitterly held to a contract he thought null and void, and after another ten years and a few studio realignments, the film was finally made, a "true story," in which Ruth Harkness sets off to China, as the actress who portrays her says, to finish her husband's mission, which was to prove that pandas were really wonderful animals. In reality, what her husband knew about pandas he read in a book, and he never got within 100 miles of one of the animals. In the film Ruth Harkness observes pandas in the wild and finds the panda cub herself. So much for "truth." What comes to be regarded as the truth is subject to fashion.

In their youth, Quentin Young and his older brother Jack had been *almost* famous, at least in the English-speaking communities in China. They wrote about their own exploits for various newspapers and magazines in Chinese and in English. Quentin figured prominently in the Harkness book, of course, and also in a 1940s book, *The Land of the Eye*, an account of a film crew's travels in Asia; Young served as their guide and Chinese military censor as they attempted to film the Burma Road, which the Allies were building as a backdoor supply route for Chinese forces fighting the Japanese.

Jack Young appears in two exploration classics, *Men Against the Clouds,* which follows a mountaineering expedition up Minya Konka in Sichuan, and in *Trailing the Giant Panda,* which Kermit and Theodore Roosevelt, Jr., sons of the ex-president, wrote about the expedition in which they shot what they thought was the first giant panda ever seen by Westerners. They brought that pelt and countless others back to Chicago's Field Museum, where they are still on display.

Much of Quentin and Jack Young's story is borne out in the yellowing correspondence in the archives of the Field Museum and the American Museum of Natural History in New York. But the rest comes from Quentin and Jack's memories, told out of order, and from different perspectives, because the two had been estranged for years. And sometimes the tales were edited or censored. My tape recorder would go on and off, depending on what they cared to divulge publicly and what they told me as background, so that I would understand their perspective, even if they didn't want to see it in print.

Jack lived in a rambling white house just outside of St. Louis. His living room was furnished with exquisitely carved

*Jack (left) and Quentin Young floating cages of pheasants downstream.
Courtesy June Young.*

wooden tables and chairs he'd brought back from several tours of duty as a U.S. Army intelligence officer in Asia. The pelt of a snow leopard he'd shot was draped over the back of one couch. He was spry and sparkling, already well into his eighties, and despite being born in the United States and spending most of his life in the Army, he spoke with a noticeable Chinese accent. But he was wise to everything I wanted from him.

During one interview, when I asked overly pressing questions about Quentin, he dramatically lifted the phone, fixed his steely eyes on me, and said, "Let's call him, shall we?"

He dialed the phone, and when Quentin answered at the other end the brothers chatted a moment in Chinese. Then Jack handed the receiver to me, and I made awkward small talk with Quentin—he had no idea why—before hanging up.

Later in our interview, Jack produced a photocopy of a famous photograph of a young Sun Yatsen and his revolutionary associates, pointed to a robed man with a Mandarin queue, and proudly told me that it was his grandfather, Yang Holin, one of Dr. Sun's closest confidantes.

A week or so later, I showed the picture to Quentin Young, telling him how impressed I was. Quentin looked at the picture through his reading glasses and let out a breathy huff, then told me he was tired and wanted to rest.

The next day, Quentin tossed the picture on a coffee table in front of me, then opened a Chinese history book to a similar photograph. In fact, it was the same photograph, but whereas Jack's version showed five men sitting next to each other, Quentin's showed only four. The fifth had been edited out for political reasons he didn't care to explain.

"This is not my grandfather," he growled, pointing to the man Jack had fingered. "My grandfather was Young Tak Cho, and he *was* an associate of Dr. Sun."

"I don't know why my brother says such things," Quentin then said, and perhaps to suggest that he really did know, he pulled out a Christmas card he'd received from Jack, suggesting they talk on the telephone before either met with me, just to make sure they got their stories straight.

The two brothers barely talked, and when Jack died of lymphoma in October, 2000, Quentin did not go east for the funeral. As Quentin aged, he had several more strokes. His memory faded but his impatience burned hotter, and he started fretting about the truth as well, that Ruth Harkness's relatives might be embarrassed by the details of his intimate relationship with her, that he'd been too hard on Jack, and that Jack would be upset. The truth can be unsettling, but as he had said during that first conversation, "The truth is the truth. Now, what else do you want to know?"

CHAPTER THREE

A CHINESE EVOLUTION

Quentin Young was born adrift, literally, on a ship in international waters, just a few days out of Hong Kong. It was 1914, and his family was returning to China after two generations in America. Jack and two other older brothers had been born in Hawaii. Later in life, when he had already moved to the United States, Quentin could not prove that he had been born to American parents because there was no record of his floating, stateless birth. It might have been an omen, because he spent his whole life adrift between two cultures, not entirely Chinese, but not quite American, either.

The Young brothers were something in between, taller than most Chinese, and they usually dressed like Americans. They had been educated in English-language schools, but their Chinese faces meant that they had to heed the odious signs they'd seen in parks in European sections of Shanghai saying "No Dogs or Chinese Allowed." Once, after he'd earned recognition as a naturalist, Jack was asked to give a speech to an English-speaking gathering of great men. He deliberately dressed in the long, flowing gowns of traditional Chinese formal wear for the event, and consequently, when he arrived at the lecture hall, the club's doorman insisted he enter by the back door like the rest of the Chinese employees.

The Young family lived in Chinese cities, not among other Chinese, but rather in the foreign concessions where Americans and Europeans had their own communities and followed their own laws, enforced by their own police departments. As children, Quentin and Jack Young read cowboy novels, but also books about great Asian explorers. Their parents bought them guitars and guns and sewing machines from the Montgomery Ward catalog, like any American family of the time that lived far away from city stores.

"Because we are different from people who lived generations in China and had never been outside of the country, our family considered themselves as higher than the others," Quentin Young told me. "They are educated people; they have been outside in the world. My father always thought that foreign education was very important, so he put us in American schools."

Even their names were lost between cultures. The family name was Yang, which, fittingly, means "overseas." Their grandfather changed the English spelling to more closely approximate the Chinese pronunciation. Otherwise it came out *Yang,* rhymes with "twang," rather than *Yang* rhymes with "tong."

In business with English-speakers, their father, Young Tung, called himself F.T. Young. Quentin was named Tilin at birth, but his English-speaking teachers couldn't tolerate Chinese names. They'd renamed one of his older brothers Albert, and then when Tai Jack came along, they renamed him Wilbert. Tilin, the youngest of the three, became Elbert. The teachers probably thought this was amusing—the "-bert" brothers.

But when Tai Jack came back from his travels with the Roosevelts, he came back as Jack Theodore Young, and Tilin followed suit with the name of another Roosevelt brother: Quentin, a war hero whose plane had been shot down by Germans during World War I. They faced the rest of their long lives bearing the names they chose for themselves.

Young Tak Cho, the family patriarch and Quentin and Jack's grandfather, was born in 1858, in Cui Heng, in the South China province of Guangdong. Like many young Chinese men of his generation, he migrated to San Francisco, partly to seek his fortune in the Golden State.

A generation of Chinese had already been lured there by the California Gold Rush that began in the 1850s. The Chinese referred to California as "Gold Mountain," but when they got there, they found more work as fishermen and laborers than as gold miners. Chinese workers were instrumental in building railroads. As they prospered, they became merchants and restaurateurs, and that prosperity raised eyebrows.

By the 1870s, the California economy had taken a downturn, and unemployed Californians voiced their resentment over the Chinese immigrants. They disliked that the Chinese sent their wages home to China rather than spending them in California. They disparaged Chinese culture, labeling the new immigrants as depraved and prone to the worst vices.

"They do not come to settle or make homes, and not one in fifty of them is married," reads an 1874 real estate circular. "Their women are all suffering slaves and prostitutes, for which possession murderous feuds and high-handed cruelty are constantly occurring. To compare the Chinese with even the lowest white laborers is, therefore, absurd."

Such strong feelings led to the Chinese Exclusion Act in 1882, which severely limited Asian immigration. It's little wonder that Young Tak Cho soon left San Francisco for Hawaii to take a job with an old friend from his ancestral village. At that time, Hawaii was still an island kingdom; it became a republic in 1893, and then was annexed by the United States in 1898, which brought the Chinese Exclusion Act to its shores, too.

But persons of Chinese ancestry were well treated there. Given its location in the Pacific, it was a stopover for ships crossing between China and the United States. Chinese and Japanese immigrants intermarried with Hawaiians. And they were the first to cultivate sugar cane on the islands.

Young Tak Cho worked for Sun Mei, a wealthy landowner who had a plantation on the big island of Hawaii, growing rice and grazing cattle. He was also the older brother and principal financial supporter of Dr. Sun Yatsen, who had spent his teenage years in his brother's care.

Young Tak Cho managed the Sun ranch, and according to Quentin Young, later helped manage the finances of Dr. Sun's revolution, as well.

Sun Yatsen left Hawaii in 1883 to finish his studies in China because his older brother worried that if he were to study on the mainland United States, he would convert to Christianity.

Quentin and Jack's father, Young Tung, was born that same year, and grew up "a cowboy," as Quentin put it. In 1900, when he was 17, Young Tung journeyed to China to find a suitable Chinese bride. His new wife, Chen Shi, was a traditional Buddhist woman with bound feet, a mark of her upper-class status. She'd been educated by a tutor who sat behind a screen to prevent his gazing upon her features and compromising her virtues. And as a woman of substance, when she came to Hawaii, she brought two slaves with her, a nursemaid and a cook. Upon the newlyweds' return to Hawaii, Young Tung took a job in the commissary of a tobacco company in Honolulu, and later managed a general store on the island of Kona.

The year Young Tung found his bride in China was the year China's ongoing struggle with the West came to a head. Foreigners had been a source of both inspiration and resentment for the Chinese through most of the nineteenth century. In the 1840s and 1850s, the Chinese rulers tried to keep English merchants from smuggling opium into the country, and Great Britain responded with military force. As a result of the Opium Wars, China ceded Hong Kong to Great Britain, as well as "concessions" in several port cities, including Shanghai.

The more conservative and patriotic elements of Chinese society saw the influx of Christian missionaries as a threat to traditional religion and culture. And while the Chinese economy had been agrarian, European and American entrepreneurs were digging mines and building industries at Chinese expense—all of it watched over by foreign military forces.

In 1900, China exploded with the anti-foreigner uprisings that Westerners called the Boxer Rebellion because its soldiers were members of martial arts societies. The Western powers called it a rebellion, but in truth, the Empress Dowager, the power behind the throne of the Manchu rulers, the Qing family, supported the Boxers.

In a rampage, the Boxers killed Western diplomats in Beijing, and the West responded by sending troops to squash the "rebels." Soldiers from the United States, Italy, Great Britain, Russia, Japan, and later Germany easily defeated the Boxers, most of whom shunned firearms, relying instead on imagined magic powers and righteousness.

The rout was humiliating for China. The Qing Dynasty had been in power for more than 200 years, but that power was fading fast, especially when the Western powers extracted punishment: Chinese military forces were cut, Western military presence strengthened. And the indemnity extracted crushed the Chinese economy.

Increasingly, China became a stage where the Western powers acted out their disputes elsewhere in the world. Japan and Russia both eyed Manchuria to expand their territories and even fought a war over it. Big cities, like Shanghai, were wide-open and bustling, their commerce dominated by Europeans and Americans who lived in their own little sub-cities, or concessions, where Chinese officials had no authority.

If Western domination fostered resentment, Western ideas were a source of inspiration. Millions of Chinese who had been educated abroad were returning to China. The work of philosophers such as Mill and Montesquieu were being translated into Chinese, and so were the novels of Dickens and other writers. Chinese intelligentsia, hungry for modernization, studied the late nineteenth century unifications of Germany and Italy. They started talking about "inalienable rights," and freedom and gender equality—and about keeping China for Chinese. They longed to be invulnerable again, and they needed power and wealth to get there, so it's no wonder that Dr. Sun's party would be referred to in the West as "Nationalist."

Sun was living in Japan, traveling the world, drumming up support for his revolution. Back home in China, there was a series of uprisings against the Manchu court, the last of them, in 1911, successful enough that Sun raced back to China from Denver, Colorado after he read about it in a local daily newspaper.

Sun was elected provisional president of the newly created republic, though he was president in name only, because that republic was not yet in control of China. He presided for less than two months. When the Qing court abdicated, a politician named Yuan Shikai stepped forward and made himself president. Sun resigned his titular post.

But with the new republic established, Jack and Quentin Young's grandfather, Young Tak Cho decided to return to his native land and settled into the ancestral village. Young Tung, their father, stayed in Hawaii, but in 1914, with world war inching closer to the United States, he decided to move his four children and his pregnant wife to China, as well.

By then, the fledgling republic under Yuan Shikai was pushing to unify the entire country—the coastal parts, at least, and ward off the Japanese threat in Manchuria to the Northeast.

But it was a good time for overseas Chinese like the Youngs. Dr. Sun had been a strong influence on China; he and his brothers had spent time in the West, after all. And the Young family, like other overseas Chinese, was caught up in the excitement of the modern world, one that fused the new sciences with ancient tradition. Darwin's theory of evolution had reached China, and "survival of the fittest" was a concept that modern Chinese intelligentsia could hold up as a metaphor for their new nation's potential.

Young Tung's brother was a mining engineer, educated at Yale and Lehigh Universities. He'd been hired to run an iron mine outside Hankow (now called Wuhan). Young Tung worked in the English concession of that city and lived in an elegant old house in the French concession.

He only held the job about a year. In 1915, President Yuan signed The Twenty-one Demands, a lopsided agreement with the Japanese government, one event in a series of ongoing diplomatic bullying. Under conditions of one of the demands, the mine was turned over to Japanese managers.

Young Tung opened an auto parts store in Hankow, and that is where Jack and Quentin Young grew up. Young Tung's brother opened a car dealership in Shanghai; because of their American citizenship, the elder Young brothers were able to get cooperation from U.S. suppliers.

Young Tung and Chen Shi had six children, four sons and two daughters. In 12 years of conversations, Quentin Young never referred to his sisters, except in the abstract; one was born in Hawaii, the other in China, and they lived out their lives in China. And his first two brothers were so much older than he that they were less like siblings and more like disapproving uncles. They ordered him around, and in the end, he did not know them well.

Sun, the oldest, was born in 1902, and he was consequently the first to return to the United States to study political science at Georgetown University, with the idea of getting a government job in China. The Chinese government assigned him to a lowly consular post in South America, which he felt was beneath him. He married the niece of a warlord who got him a professorship at a local university, but when the warlord fell, he lost his job. As a member of the liberal party, he couldn't find favor with Chiang Kaishek's Kuomintang or with the Communists. Quentin last heard from him in the 1950s, in a letter postmarked from Hong Kong, where Sun was looking for political asylum. He disappeared afterward, obviously having angered one side or the other.

Brother Albert was born in 1907. When he was 15, he repeatedly annoyed his parents by throwing parties at restaurants and sending the bill to his mother. So he was packed off to live with relatives in San Francisco and clean up his act. He became a chef and a freelance writer and bit of a scalawag. Quentin only came to know him years later.

When they were all old men reunited in the U.S., Jack Young told me, Albert claimed he had been houseboy to the writer Dorothy Parker. During late-night conversations with Jack, Albert would point to passages in Parker's work and say that in fact, *he* had written them while Parker was drunk and on deadline.

Jack was born in 1910, the last of the Young brothers born in Hawaii. Quentin was born in 1914. His earliest memory is of chasing dragonflies in the gardens near the family's home. He'd catch them, tie pieces of yarn to their heads, then release them and watch them fly off, trailing color behind them like a flag.

And when he was three or four, while hunting dragonflies, he fell into a small pond and nearly drowned. A passing neighbor saw his lifeless body floating in the shallow water among the weeds near shore and at first thought it was a dead pig. He went down for a closer look, and then he pulled the little boy from the pond, pumped the water from his lungs and took him home.

Though they were four years apart, Jack and Quentin were constant companions as children. They were both precocious, taught by tutors at home, and they skipped grade school altogether and started in junior high school at the age of nine. And they were co-conspirators.

Quentin recalled a day when the French children living across the street shot bb guns toward the Young house while shooting at birds. Jack and Quentin retaliated with their own bb guns, shooting the French family's drainpipes full of holes so that the French father came over to have an angry word with Mr. and Mrs. Young.

They must have been competent young fellows, because even as teenagers, their parents would allow them to travel alone up the Yangsi river to go camping in the province of Sikong, which has since been absorbed into Sichuan. That back country experience would greatly play into their futures.

In 1927, Jack received a scholarship from the local missionary school to attend New York University and study journalism. Quentin didn't hear much from him, but Jack would send him postage stamps for a collection they kept.

"Oh, I had a good time with those stamps," Quentin told me.

In June of 1929, when Quentin was 15, Jack showed up unexpectedly in Hankow, on his way back to New York from an 18-month expedition with the Roosevelt brothers. No one even knew he had gone. To Quentin's delight, he had with him a steamer trunk full of documents and animal skins and jars of shrews pickled in formaldehyde. He had a Colt automatic pistol, and a .22 rifle that could be unscrewed and disassembled to fit into the trunk. Jack had used it to collect birds and small mammals in the field.

"This is the real thing," Jack told Quentin. "It's not for kids."

Then he took his younger brother down into their basement, which ran under the length of their long narrow house, and taught him to shoot the rifle.

"It sounded big and loud," Quentin recalled. And it left an impression.

Jack stayed long enough in Hankow to write a lengthy account of his journey for the English-language journal, *The China Weekly Review*, then returned to New York and new adventures.

The family did not stay in Hankow much longer because Young Tung's business had been wiped out. Dr. Sun had longed to regain power, but when he died in 1926, his political heir, Chiang Kaishek, controlled the republic's military. In 1927 and 1928, Chiang and his Northern Expedition Forces had swept through the region to drive out the remaining warlords and unify China under the Nationalist government.

As the warlord's troops retreated, they cleaned out Young Tung's automotive supply store, paying with military bank notes they'd printed themselves. Young Tung tried to raise prices to discourage the purchases, but the soldiers bought parts anyway. He thought he'd be able to convert the military notes into better currency, but the warlord fell so fast that he never got the chance. So Young Tung packed up what family was left in Hankow—his wife, Quentin and his younger sister—and moved to the ancestral village, Cui Heng.

Unfortunately, there were no schools Quentin could attend there. In 1930, at the age of 16, he traveled to Shanghai to study at a government teacher training institute. When he finished, he returned to Cui Heng to teach mathematics, physical education, English, and Mandarin Chinese—the local dialect was Cantonese—to students who were sometimes older than he. He planned to save his money to attend junior college in Shanghai and then get an even better job teaching high school.

But his interest in science and discovery had been piqued by Jack's adventure with the Roosevelts, and he set out on a learning quest of his own. He read every book he could find about zoology. There were none written in Chinese, however, and in order to read about the wealth of species China had to offer, he had to buy books in English and Japanese. None of the books had stories about giant pandas.

Biology was his favorite subject, and he was a bit of a teacher's pet to the instructor, a bespectacled young Chinese man of about 20. Among his interminable questions, Quentin wanted to know why everything he learned about China he had to learn from foreign books. The instructor was agreeable and encouraging, and in the new nationalism of the day he told Quentin that the Chinese should indeed write such things for themselves.

Darwinism, genetics: It was an exciting time to be studying such modern theories. Genetic variety required a large enough gene pool within species to prevent inbreeding; variety in breeding made the offspring stronger. This is what Quentin learned. And so he suggested to the teacher that humans could do the same by intermingling the races.

The teacher answered with a worried smile. It was a good thought, he told the younger man. The idea had merit. But, he concluded, China probably wasn't ready for such a modern idea as that. But as for what a Chinese could do for science and his country, well, that was a different matter altogether.

CHAPTER FOUR

JACK

Jack and Quentin Young were poster boys for "The New China," taller and more modern-looking than most Chinese, favoring slick, black pompadours and Western suits. They were hybrids from the same seeds, but different in personality.

Jack was the shorter of the two, more wiry, and so charming that he could talk a bird from the tree into a cage. And as the older brother, he always went first, making a smashing first impression wherever he went and then boasting of his accomplishments.

Quentin was tall and so introspective that he was almost brooding, and while Jack charged ahead, Quentin was blown here and there in his wake. With equal parts admiration and competitive jealousy, Quentin felt compelled to follow in Jack's footsteps—trying to take bigger steps than Jack had. But more often than not through their long lives, Jack's trailblazing would just wake the snakes along the trail. He'd hike happily on, and Quentin, following behind, would be bitten. And when Jack chose the exotic profession of naturalist, Quentin had to follow. It came by accident.

To help pay his expenses as a college student in New York, Jack found a part-time job at the Chinese legation in Manhattan, and he was working there in the fall of 1928 when Kermit and Theodore Roosevelt, Jr., came in to secure visas for the William V. Kelley-Roosevelts Field Museum Expedition to South China.

The sons of the late president were businessmen in their 30s; Ted was also a statesmen. They were dashing and decorated veterans of World War I, like their brother Quentin, who had been shot down in an air battle. Theodore would go on to be governor of Puerto Rico and of the Philippines; as a brigadier general, he would personally lead one of the first assaults on Normandy Beach during World War II, then die of a heart attack on the battlefield in Normandy before that campaign ended.

Kermit Roosevelt was less illustrious than Theodore Jr., reputed to be of a darker temperament, and given to heavy drinking. (He too would die of a heart attack while in the Army during World War II, but at a remote station in Alaska, rather than on the battlefield.)

They'd been on safari with their famous father and had already staged an expedition to Central Asia. They were fashionably smitten with wanderlust, and they had the wealth and the connections to live their fantasies. Like the rest of the Great White Hunters, they were men of romantic affectation, bored with their tame upper-class lives and looking for exotic wild places to explore.

Near the beginning of their book *Trailing the Giant Panda,* Ted writes of his and Kermit's mutual longing to go traveling, of their lunches with like-minded souls, "the brown lean men who drift quietly into New York, not those who go tourist-like across Africa in automobiles, camping each night in richly upholstered luxury, but [adventurers] who trek to lonely places where food is scant, travel by foot, and danger a constant bedfellow.

"Almost without realizing it we started to discuss where we should go next. Naturally we turned to the blank spaces on the map, those fascinating white blotches with perhaps the dotted course of a surmised river marked and 'unknown' printed across them. These are much fewer now than they were twenty years ago, but such as they are they beckon just as irresistibly."

The areas they ended up visiting were in fact peopled, but they hadn't been truly "explored," that is, visited by sophisticated white folks other than some few American and European missionaries in remote outposts.

In those days, travel meant more than just *being* somewhere else. There was no boarding a jet and waking up a half day later on the other side of the world, checking into a luxury hotel with a parking lot overlooking one of the seven wonders, then being met at the tour bus by a guide wearing a Puff Daddy T-shirt and listening to a Walkman stereo. Back then, travel could take months, even years, giving the traveler time to reflect on the gradual change of scenery from the deck of a ship, the window of a train, or the saddle.

Travel in China might as well have been time travel. There were still tribes of remote and authentically primitive peoples, still unseen places. There were still strange and exotic animal species to name and heroically kill to be mounted in a glass case in some museum in New York or Chicago or London, or better yet, to capture alive and exhibit in an American or European zoo.

Of course even the Roosevelts were not wealthy enough—or not willing, at least—to travel there on their own bank accounts, and so they asked the relatively young Field Museum to find donors to foot the bill, which also included a hefty paycheck for the brothers. And in return they would bring back specimens to fill a new Asian hall in the museum.

Meeting Jack Young was good luck for everyone involved. The Roosevelts needed a Chinese interpreter. They'd hoped to engage an Asian actor named Kru, who had starred in a 1927 silent film about a Thai family whose rice fields were trampled by a lovable rogue elephant named Chang. But Kru was unavailable, having become a missionary and gone off to save souls in some distant corner of Asia. It was pure good fortune they stumbled upon Jack Young, who happily told them how many dialects he spoke and of the trips he and Quentin had taken to some of the very same areas the Roosevelts hoped to visit.

"We knew that country like the palm of our hand from when we were in high school," Jack Young told me. "I said, 'I will go. I know where it is.'"

The Roosevelts were as impressed with Jack Young as they were hard up. They described Young in their book as "a nice-looking boy about 20 years old." In fact he was only 18, and it would be no surprise if he lied to them to get himself on the trip.

On October 4, 1928, Kermit Roosevelt fired off a telegram to Dr. SC Simms, president of the Field Museum.

"Young Chinaman who although American born has spent all his life in China and has been in Yunnan and Szechuan is most anxious join expedition as interpreter and ready to do any sort of work to justify his going. He is recommended by Chinese ambassador," he wrote.

You can almost hear Simms sighing in his responding telegram:

"Doubt if Chinaman can be trained in two weeks to be of value to the expedition," he wrote back. "If for diplomatic reasons you consider taking him, send him on and will do the best with him in the allotted time."

A day later, Young left New York for Chicago carrying a letter of introduction to Dr. Simms. Kermit Roosevelt had given him travel money and asked if Simms would put him up. Young spent the next two weeks learning to prepare specimens, and on October 31, he set sail from New York listed as an attendant to 565 mules being shipped to India on the freighter Egremont. He landed in Karachi and made his way intrepidly alone to Calcutta to await the rest of the party.

Meanwhile, the Roosevelts traveled through Europe, stopping to hobnob with old friends and fellow naturalists. On December 14, they reached Rangoon, and met up with other expedition principals, a New York businessman named C. Suydam Cutting and a British ornithologist named Herbert Stevens. With everyone present and accounted for, the expedition steamed up the Irawaddy River to Mandalay and Bhamo, then motored and took trains to the Burmese border with China, and finally set out afoot with a caravan of porters and mules.

The trail carried them through villages separated by vast tracts of wilderness, up over high passes, through jungles and pine forests. At times the trail was less than a foot wide. At times it was so cold at night that the mules would flee for lower and warmer altitudes, and the porters would have to go off in search of them at dawn's light.

At around four each afternoon, when they quit the trail, Jack Young would lay out lines of traps for squirrels and shrews and other small mammals. He would gather droppings and flora and fauna from the animals' habitats. At night he'd skin and otherwise prepare what he'd caught and killed, making the specified measurements so that taxidermists would be able to accurately mount the skins later, what Young called "measuring him for a suit, but you've taken his coat from him."

His other great responsibility was to travel ahead of the expedition to the next village and find the magistrate. There he'd present the Roosevelts' calling cards and arrange for safe passage and fresh coolies to get them as far as the next municipality, where another magistrate would assign more porters for the next stretch.

The Roosevelts worried constantly about bandits—what they called "the bugaboo of brigandage" in this lawless corner of China—and often when they entered a village, they had arrived just after the bandits had carried off something or someone. At times the magistrates sent soldiers to accompany them; once Jack witnessed the beheading of two young bandits who had been captured. And at least once, the Roosevelt caravan had a stand-down with armed men they met along the trail.

Jack felt he was an integral part of the expedition. "Considering the era, [the Roosevelts] were most open-minded," he told me. "There was no discrimination. I shared the same tent with them."

The racism is subtle in *Trailing the Giant Panda*. The white men are usually referred to by last names; Jack Young is simply "Jack." Chinese locals are patronized throughout. For example, Kermit took ill one night and Jack Young was dispatched to find a local doctor—whom the Roosevelts ridiculed. They were amused by the "king" of a small village, amused that the village could call itself a kingdom. And when they traveled through such villages, they were all described simply as being "Chinese."

But even to Jack Young, the only westernized Chinese among them, these places were strange and foreign. He reacted as if he were visiting another planet, which he might as well have been doing. In his own writings about the adventure, he, too, made fun of peasant superstitions, such as the alleged monster living in a rushing river that was said to surge up and carry unsuspecting bridge-crossers to their deaths.

Though Young spoke English with a fairly thick Chinese accent, the account he published in *The China Weekly Review*, right after the expedition, was delightfully fluent, written in the jaunty and romantic style of travel writing in the first half of the twentieth century. Young was a breathless and enthusiastic anthropologist when he described the native peoples he encountered.

"These Tibetans are men of splendid physique and great strength, and are frequently more than six feet in height," he wrote. "They have brick-red complexions and some are really handsome in a full blooded masculine way. They wear fur caps and long loose coats like Russian blouses thrown carelessly off one shoulder and tied about the waist, blue or red trousers, and high boots of felt or skin reaching almost to the knees. A long sword, its hilt inlaid with bright bits of stones, is half concealed beneath their coats, and they are seldom without a gun or some murderous looking weapon. [. . .]

"We had three Tibetan muleteers. They were picturesque, jolly, and wild-looking fellows. In their swinging walk, there is a care-free independence and an atmosphere of bleak Tibetan steppes which are strangely fascinating. In the breast of the loose coat which acts as a pocket, they carry a remarkable assortment of things, a pipe, tobacco, tea, tsamba [roasted barley, a Tibetan food staple], and hanging down in front, a metal charm box with a Buddha inside it to protect them from bullets and sickness."

His description was just as colorful a few pages later when he encountered the Lolo peoples (now called the Yi) who lived in log homes in Sichuan and could "move noiselessly through the weird, somber pine forest.

"These Lolo are tall and fierce looking fellows with comparatively fair complexions, and often with straight features, suggesting a mixture of Mongolian with some straight-featured race. The Lolos say of themselves that they came from the direction of Burma. 'They consider a man who captures another man to be a man; a man who allows himself to be captured only half a man,' remarked General Pereira in his book, *From Peking to Lhassa*. Like almost every tribe which has been conquered by the Chinese or has come into continual contact with them for a few generations, these Lolos are being absorbed by the Chinese. I found that in some instances they were giving up their language and talk Chinese even among themselves. Some women had already begun to tie up their feet in the ancient Chinese fashion, and even disliked to be called Lolos."

While Jack was generally interested and admiring of the people he encountered, the Roosevelts tended to dismiss them. For example, they hired a tribal headman, the region's best hunter, who was shocked when he realized that the Roosevelts actually killed their own animals. For him, the hunt was the important and prestigious part; the actual killing was dirty work best delegated to underlings. He might have had a point, but the Roosevelts turned the joke around, laughing that anyone could think so mistakenly of their chosen avocation.

The Roosevelts' amusement sometimes lapsed into arrogance. There is a chilling scene in their book in which they shot a family of what they called golden monkeys (and the biologist George Schaller suggests might have been Tibetan macaques). One of the dead monkeys that fell from a tree was "as big as an eight-year-old child." But even while the brothers were happily annihilating primate families, they were incensed when their native hunters started firing, too, scandalized, even, when the heathens killed a monkey themselves. Even if the Field Museum lent its prestigious name to this so-called scientific expedition, clearly the Roosevelts were not scientists gathering species for the advancement of zoology. They were sportsmen out on a hunt. Collecting for the Field Museum was a way to get someone else to pay for the adventure.

The giant panda was bigger game. Jack Young referred to it in his article as "the sportsman's prize above all others worth working hard for in Western China." When the Roosevelts reached panda country, they sought out hunters who had shot the animals, and were a bit surprised to find so few. And those men had not actually hunted the pandas, but rather shot them because they were marauding through a village or raiding someone's bee hives. One hunter had shot his panda when it wandered into his camp looking for a handout after it had smelled the pork bones he was cooking. When the hunter suggested to the Roosevelts that they cook some bones to see if they could lure another panda out of the forest, the Roosevelts indulged him so as not to anger him, but called the suggestion "rankest folly."

Several times, the team split in two groups. Young and Cutting took the low route, looking for small game. The Roosevelts took the high route in search of takin and panda.

On April 13, 1929, the Roosevelts found fresh panda sign. There was stiff white hair caught on the bark of trees and scat filled with undigested bamboo. This was the first evidence of pandas that the Roosevelts had seen. They found panda tracks and followed them uphill through nearly impassable bamboo thickets. As Jack Young told me, "Once you get into bamboo, then Lord help you, because you can't even see from here to there. And this guy, the panda, has a way of wriggling his behind, and he gets over there faster than you can ever dream." And as Quentin Young confirmed, "You see a flash of black and white and it's gone."

The snow was wet and heavy, and the trail seemed to grow cold. Just as the Roosevelt brothers decided to split in separate directions, one of the Lolo hunters gestured to them and pointed to where a giant panda was coming out of the hollow of a large spruce tree. Kermit saw it first and motioned to Ted. The panda walked unhurriedly into the bamboo. Both brothers fired. The panda fled, wounded, and the brothers trailed it for 75 yards until it collapsed, dead.

(Quentin Young, whose own panda capture was called into doubt, questioned if the Roosevelts really fired simultaneously.

"Ted Roosevelt said they shot the panda at the same time," he said. Then referring to his own feat, continued, "It's the same thing. But *he* is a Roosevelt, and so what *he* told you was correct." And by extension, what the Chinese man said is always questionable.)

Kermit slithered the seven miles downhill to camp to get a camera to record the kill and mules to cart the carcass back to camp. Ted and the Lolo had tried to float it down a stream and failed, and then decided to gut it right there in the forest. The other Lolos did not want to allow the dead panda in their camp, but they relented for the Roosevelts. Afterwards, they called in a priest to purify the area after the panda was removed.

Jack Young saw the animal two days later when the two factions of the expedition reunited, and he described it in his article. "The Panda that the Roosevelts shot was a beautiful specimen," he wrote, "weighing more than two hundred pounds. He had a thick white coat of fur with black splotches. His head was white with black fringes of hair around the eyes. According to the Roosevelts, the Panda is believed to be a member of the bear family, but unlike the bear, it never hibernates in the winter and has 42 teeth instead of 40. Otherwise it is quite similar to the bear species."

The Roosevelts continued on to Yunnan and then took the train for Indochina. When they reached Hanoi on May 14, the brothers Roosevelt sent a triumphant telegram to the Field Museum:

"Have had extraordinary luck. Jointly shot for you splendid old male Giant Pandar," they wrote, "Believe authorities agree this is the first Giant Pandar shot by white man." They spelled "panda" with an extra "r," phonetically, as they would undoubtedly have pronounced it with their aristocratic accents.

In seven months, they had walked nearly a thousand miles. And when they finally lurched out of the jungle, Cutting and the Roosevelts had long dark explorers' beards. Kermit left Hanoi for the United States. Ted stayed in Indochina to meet up with the other part of the expedition, which was still cutting its way across Indochina. When they were finally done, they brought 12,633 specimens back to Chicago, including plants, reptiles and amphibians, insects and mammals. There were five pandas among the specimens: one the Roosevelts shot and others that they bought from local hunters.

Jack Young first traveled to Hankow to see his family. When he returned to New York, he had a few thousand dollars in his pocket and he had earned the titles of "naturalist" and "adventurer." These, he thought, might be better career choices than that of "journalist," and so he decided to finish out the year at NYU and then transfer to the University of Chicago, provided he could get a part-time job at the Field Museum. He wrote several letters to curators there. Kermit Roosevelt wrote on his behalf, and the chief curator recommended him to the president, but the appointment never came.

In the meantime, given his new status as an adventurer, Young had taken to visiting the Explorers Club in Manhattan, and like the Roosevelts, he soon found himself plotting his next adventure.

When *Trailing the Giant Panda* was published, Jack Young noted in a letter to a friend that it didn't really say very much about animals. He was right: it was travelogue. But Young and his friends couldn't help but remark on a few sentences in the book about a certain mountain the Roosevelts had seen along the route. The Roosevelts called it "Mount Koonka"—a mispronunciation of the Tibetan name, Minya Konka—and they repeated hearsay that it was more than 30,000 feet tall, which would make it higher than Everest. The adventuring community took notice.

In the late 1920s and early 1930s, science and adventure journals were full of speculative articles about the world's tallest mountains. Minya Konka, which the Chinese now call Gonga Shan, was a candidate, and so were other peaks in the Amne Machin range of West Central China. In 1930, a group at the Explorers Club set for themselves the modest goal of determining and then scaling the world's highest peak.

Jack Young surrounded by his companions from the 1932 Minya Konka expedition. Courtesy June Young.

Jack Young was approached in 1931, not for his mountaineering skills, for he had none, but for his knowledge of the area, for his reputation for fearlessness, and of course for his connections, not just with the Chinese government, but with Colonel Ted Roosevelt, who was already Governor General of the Philippines.

The expedition had the support of the American Geographical Society of New York, and after being stalled when the Japanese invaded Manchuria in the fall of 1931, finally arrived in Shanghai in January, 1932. There were nine expeditionaries, initially. They were doctors and engineers and students from Ivy League colleges; things quickly went wrong for the expedition, and most of them never made it out of Shanghai.

On January 28, the nine of them were lunching in a Shanghai hotel room when the doors leading to the room's balcony blew open from the concussion of the first explosions of the Japanese invasion of Shanghai. They climbed to the hotel's roof and watched a Japanese battleship fire shells point-blank into the Chinese sectors of the city from the harbor. Moments later, bomber planes flew overhead and dropped their payloads. Machine gun fire erupted from the Japanese concession of the city as troops there made their move.

The Americans dutifully reported to U.S. Marine headquarters in Shanghai and were issued guns and helmets and armbands and put to work patrolling the American-held parts of the city. Jack Young disappeared.

Terris Moore later wrote in the book *Men Against the Clouds*, "During the third night, in the gloomiest part of my patrol beat, a startling but familiar voice spoke out of the darkness: 'Hey, Terry? Let me have a handful of cartridges?' It was Jack Young. I thought quickly. Why of course, he's firing from the Chinese side, badly needing ammunition. As an experienced hunter from the Roosevelt expedition, doubtless *he* knows how to make each shot count! We had been issued thirty rounds apiece, but not being engaged ourselves, we had not fired any. Wondering what excuse to give later for the missing rounds, I handed Jack ten, and he promptly disappeared."

The Japanese did not venture into Shanghai's foreign concessions, but with the fighting going on, it became clear that the expedition was going nowhere soon. The expedition members booked passage on a steamer to Nanjiang to get out of harm's way and ponder the next move from there.

Several returned home. Others got messages to relatives in the States who told them that since the American economy was so poor and the cost of living was cheap in China, that they might as well stay put. Jack suggested that his companions spend their time learning to speak Chinese.

In the end, the expedition boiled down to four: Young; a 22-year-old graduate student named Terris Moore (who later became president of the University of Alaska); Arthur Emmons, an engineering student in his junior year at Harvard; and Richard Burdsall, a 30-something engineer. They called themselves the Sikong Expedition, taking the name from the newly formed province of Sikong, because that's where they were headed.

"Sikong" meant "Western Kong," named after the people who lived there, the "Kang," or "Kong" (now spelled, "Qiang)," an ethnic group related to Tibetans and other western Chinese indigenous peoples. It was once called "Inner Tibet," and has since been absorbed into Sichuan.

Though local Chinese government authorities worried that this Sikong Expedition was going to sneak through China and Tibet to reach Everest, the expedition members had already scuttled those plans as impractical and set as their new goal a first ascent of Minya Konka to determine its altitude once and for all. Young took care of wangling the necessary permits out of the government and made an agreement to collect animal species for the Metropolitan Museum of the Academia Sinica, a national museum located in Nanjiang.

In June, Emmons and Burdsall boarded a steamer up the Yangsi, leaving Moore and Young behind to take care of the last details. River travel was the most common way to get inland, but it was not without its dangers. The steamers had to fight the strong current as they made their way upriver. And the pilots had to dodge potshots from bandits onshore.

In Chonqing, Emmons and Burdsall met Floyd Tangier Smith—Ruth Harkness and Quentin Young's nemesis in years to come. Smith was collecting for the Field Museum, and he was putting one of his Chinese assistants on the return boat for Shanghai with a pair of red pandas. Because red pandas are small and look rather like raccoons, the Ivy League boys mistook them for wildcats. Smith then took the expeditionaries into the city and showed them its English-speaking denizens.

Burdsall and Emmons boarded another steamer up the Min River to Chengdu, an isolated city, but one that had a burgeoning population of about 400,000. From there, they caravaned to Tatsienlu (now called Kangding), and up into the mountains where they established their base camp at a lamasery.

Young and Moore showed up some weeks later. Moore had tales to tell about Young's further cowboy exploits. One night while they were camped on a high pass beyond Tatsienlu, a contingent of Tibetan soldiers snuck into camp, intimidated the coolies, and made off with a horse. Young and Moore slept through the incident. The coolies, who were from that region, were used to such abuses and let the theft go unchallenged.

But Young was incensed when he woke up and learned of the theft, and the next morning he recruited a posse from among his porters, mounted up and rode after the thieves, with Moore following behind. Young tracked the soldiers for several hours, just as he would have tracked a herd of animals, and when he finally overtook them, he ordered them to stop.

They kept riding. So Young let go with a few bursts of rifle fire, shooting over their heads to get their attention. That convinced them to stop. Then, as Moore held a pistol on the bandits, Young began his interrogation.

The soldiers had the horse with them, though they'd clipped its mane in an attempt to disguise it. And once Young decided which soldier had stolen it, he marched that fellow at gunpoint to the nearest magistrate and had him thrown in jail.

Through the rest of the expedition, Young served as go-between for the American climbers and the local authorities. The lamas were not happy that anyone was climbing Minya Konka, which according to *Men Against the Clouds*, they regarded as a deity, a thunder god. Young allegedly eased their minds by assuring them that the Americans had only come to pay their respects.

Young also managed the coolies—and did a fair amount of back-breaking coolie work himself—during the long ascent, as the climbers set camps at intervals up the mountain. He did not reach the summit, choosing instead to remain at a staging camp at 20,000 feet.

Moore, Burdsall and Emmons made the final assault, but then, while on bivouac at 23,000 feet, less than 2,000 feet below the summit, Emmons accidentally sliced his hand open with a knife, severing nerves, and he decided to stay behind while the other two continued.

Moore and Burdsall summited on October 28, 1932. Minya Konka, they determined, stood 24,900 feet tall and consequently was not the world's highest mountain after all. But the ascent set an altitude record for Americans, particularly since they had climbed without oxygen. And though revisionist historians of the People's Republic of China denied the expedition had succeeded, claiming their own climbers made the first ascent in 1957, the record stood for 25 years.

(In April and May of 2001, two teams of German mountaineers attempted to climb Minya Konka following the 1932

Jack Young and Richard Burdsall with trophies from the Minya Konka Valley. Courtesy June Young.

route, and were turned back by bad weather. Dr. Hartmut Bielefeldt, one of the German climbers, wrote to me that "seeing the mountain directly, I was astonished about their so 'easy' success. Possibly the weather and conditions were better in 1932."

The 1932 climbers, of course, made their ascent without the sorts of high-tech mountaineering gear available today. Instead they had wool and down clothing, canvas tents, hobnailed boots, hemp ropes and no oxygen. Yet, true to the genre, the book they wrote gamely plays down the mountain treacheries that turned away the modern adventurers.)

After conquering the summit, the other Americans left the Minya Konka area. Jack Young stayed behind to fulfill obligations to collect species for the Academia Sinica, and in his own written accounts of the hunt, he tells of sitting on the lamasery steps with field glasses, searching for Tibetan brown bears—he shot one. He spent happy hours resting in front of a tent in a meadow at 12,000 feet, watching for pheasants and reading O. Henry short stories.

When he'd shot what he could near the lamasery, he found a guide to help him circumnambulate Minya Konka. Local warfare prevented him from heading south to where the Roosevelts shot their panda, but he traveled well into Lolo territory and the tribesmen there recognized him and received him graciously— or so he writes.

In his accounts, Young was a benevolent visitor from a more advanced and modern planet. The villagers asked him to help rid their cornfields of some pesky feral pigs. In one slapstick passage, Young describes a pig that raced out of the fields pursued by a pack of village dogs. The pig was so alarmed that it crashed right through the mud walls of one Lolo hut before Young could bring it down with a few accurate shots. The cornfields were also being raided by a troop of monkeys, which he also shot. This was in the benefit of both parties: Young brought their coveted hides back to civilization for sale to the highest bidder.

On his way out of the back country, Young discovered that Emmons had been hospitalized in Yachow because he had so badly frostbitten his feet during the climb. So Young decided to return to the field until Emmons could be released. And fortuitously so, for he captured a pair of Tibetan brown bear cubs, which he brought alive to Shanghai. He had also acquired the pelt, skull and leg bones of a giant panda—and a bad case of fleas.

Quentin Young was attending junior college in Shanghai, and Jack assigned him the job of transporting the two bear cubs from their uncle's automotive business to the museum in Nanjiang where they would be displayed for the time being.

Meanwhile, Jack Young returned triumphantly to New York to finish school and to try to sell off his Minya Konka collection. Back in the States, he convinced his old friend and Roosevelt-expedition tent mate Suydam Cutting to put up $100 to buy the giant panda skin for the American Museum of Natural History in New York. The museum curator hemmed and hawed and complained that they had no money for collections—and then wrote in a letter to Cutting that they'd pulled off quite a deal in buying such a prime specimen for so little money. A couple years later they'd make a tremendous fuss over a pelt brought back by Great White Hunter Dean Sage, who also sat on the museum's board.

Jack did manage to wangle a lukewarm agreement with the American Museum that he could send specimens from his next collecting expedition to the museum for consideration. Then, with that endorsement, he returned to Shanghai and set about pitching the bear cubs to the Bronx Zoo. His stationery was already imprinted with the letterhead, "Second Sikong Expedition," and he asked the zoo managers for quick money so that he could embark on his next trip, the one he was undertaking on behalf of the American Museum. The zoo bought the cubs, also at fire sale prices, and in January, 1934, he and Quentin started the journey back up the Yangsi toward Tatsienlu.

CHAPTER FIVE

THE SIKONG EXPEDITIONS

When he was in his seventies, Quentin Young reminded me of "Funes the Memorious," a character in a short story of the same name by the Argentine writer Jorge Luis Borges.

As a young man, Funes had suffered a head injury that made his memory so acute that he took in millions more details than any normal human. He needed hours and hours to process the memory of any given second, and finally, he took to bed permanently so as not to experience more things that he'd only have to go on remembering.

Young was like that. He had tried to write his own life story, but it was so overwhelming that he gave it up. Memories come out of order, by definition, and so he kept notes, and scribbled chronologies, trying to manage too much information. And as if that weren't stressful enough, he held onto a lifetime of nightmares as well, things he was afraid to divulge for personal or political reasons, and they always hovered near the surface, until one day, he decided not to talk any more about them at all. His wife was often afraid to tell him anything new, for fear that he would become unduly aggravated and suffer another stroke.

A Tibetan slave girl. Courtesy June Young.

During the time we spent together, random memories would pop out if and when the right association came along. For instance, I had taken him to see his doctor for gout in his left knee, and as we sat in the waiting room, the pain reminded him of an ordeal in 1934 or 1935, when he'd mysteriously become crippled in the same leg while hunting at high altitude in the Minya Konka area.

He was traveling alone with a porter, caught in a snowstorm, when the pain struck so hard that he was unable to walk a step farther. They took shelter in a cave and decided to wait out the storm. They had matches, but no food, and so Young sent the porter out to find some and maybe to find an able-bodied person to help carry him back to camp.

The weather worsened, and the porter couldn't make it back, so Young was stuck for several days. He shot a rabbit from the cave, but then realized he'd have to crawl through the snow to retrieve it. And even if he managed to crawl back, he probably couldn't make a fire hot enough to cook it. At those altitudes, water wouldn't even boil; he'd watch the women porters heat water for their tea of yak butter and salt, leaving the pot on the fire for a long time, and then taking it bare-handed from the fire because it never really heated up enough to burn.

Young stayed in the cave and ate snow for three or four days until the porter could finally make it back with food. The leg pain went away as mysteriously as it came, and he hiked out.

Other memories would spring to mind when he looked at the photo albums that he'd so carefully labeled against the day when he would no longer remember what they depicted.

A Tibetan woman in one shot drops her robe and exposes her breast.

"Too hot," he said breathily. "She's a slave. She doesn't care."

In another photo, Jack smiles broadly, his arm around a young woman porter who looks shyly down and to one side. They are standing on a high pass with snow all around them.

"She is more attentive to Jack than I," he says. "That's what I remember. If she's a lover, I don't know. That girl was on every trip to the Minya Konka area."

Jack and Quentin's mother never approved of this business they had with animals. She was a Buddhist, and she abhorred killing of any sort. Besides, she felt it was beneath them. They were overseas Chinese, after all, and hunters came from the lowest rungs of society, lower than farmers and laborers, almost as low as bandits. And their love of animals was most un-Chinese.

"The Chinese thought it was silly," Quentin Young told me. "If a dog was sick and you tried to cure it, they'd say, 'Why don't you let it die? It's only a dog!' I thought it was beautiful. But who cares about animals in China? They don't care about people."

Still, their mother understood that they were doing what they did for the glory of China. She chanted and prayed for her sons' deliverance, but understood when Quentin told her that it was shameful that "people from the Western world take our things," and then wrote the books telling them what those things were. She told them both to stick together with words they remembered as old men.

"He is always my little brother," Jack Young told me. "I always want to take care of him. That's what my mother told me: 'You have to take care of him.'"

And Quentin Young also recalls her words.

"If you encounter a tiger," she told him, "your best companion is your brother. He is the one who will fight for you."

Quentin, Su Lin and Jack Young on the Second Sikong Expedition.
Courtesy Mrs. Vivian Dai.

"So I always remember that," he said. "Against a tiger, nothing can be better than your own brother."

But already the resentment was building. In 1934 Quentin Young was studying physical education at East Asia College, a junior college in Shanghai. He'd wanted to attend the Central Chinese University, but he lacked the Kuomintang connections to get into it. He was studying physical education because he was inspired by Jesse Owens. But in reality, his main competition was his brother Jack, who was building quite a reputation as an adventurer. It didn't matter that Jack was regularly condescended to by the American museum curators, treated as a novelty, a smiling, hard-working foreigner, whom they liked just

The newlyweds, Jack and Su Lin Young, on their expedition honeymoon.
Quentin is at the stern. Courtesy Mrs. Vivian Dai.

fine—until it came time to open their checkbooks and pay him for his hard work.

Quentin was anxious to learn the museum trade, to make his own discoveries and write his own newspaper stories about them. So when Jack offered to take him along on his next expedition, he jumped at the chance. The college offered to give him course credit for the trip.

The Second Sikong Expedition finally left Shanghai in late spring or early summer, 1934. It consisted of Quentin and Jack, and Jack's new wife, Su Lin, who also went by the English name Adelaide and who, like Jack, had been born and educated in the United States. This would be their honeymoon.

The expedition route doubled back on the areas that Jack had hunted after climbing Minya Konka. From Chengdu, they traveled overland to Tatsienlu, crossed the Tung River at Luding, then crossed Tseimi Pass, which was higher than 15,000 feet in elevation, and established base camp at the Tibetan lamasery, Konka Gompa (now spelled Gongka Gompa), a rambling wooden building with pagoda-like eaves. The lamasery, which is still there and still occupied, stands at 10,000 feet, overlooking the river, thousands of feet below.

The terrain climbed from desert cactus to glaciers. The trail passed through pine and rhododendron and bamboo forests and high grasslands. In places, the trail was so narrow and so precipitous that they had to remove the packs from the horses to get them over safely.

When talking of the raging rivers they crossed and the dangerous trails they hiked, Jack Young once told me, "When you go there, you either come back or you don't. We never thought of it."

Su Lin strikes the pose of a huntress. Courtesy Mrs. Vivian Dai.

They always had ten or fifteen coolies, arranged by order of the central Chinese government, though it sometimes also required bribing magistrates with silk stockings and cheap dresses as gifts for their women. This method of travel was called Ullah or Ula transport, and it was only available to important people. In effect, it was a form of taxation. When a dignitary came to the village with the appropriate paperwork, the village headman was supposed to provide cooks and coolies and horses to take the dignitary and his party to the next village where they would find new porters and horses. The caravan would thus travel in stages, like those of the Pony Express.

In reality, what the Youngs found was that the villagers were not happy about being indentured. At least once, they arrived at a village to find that everyone had locked up and fled to avoid being pressed into service, taking yaks and horses, and leaving their mastiff dogs chained outside the houses as guards.

When the Youngs entered a village, they would usually hand a bullet to the headman as a symbol of their seriousness. If they had to travel through dangerous areas—and there were many, filled with bandits and anti-Chinese sentiments—they would visit the local magistrate, who would hold hostages to guarantee that the expedition would have safe passage. When they'd safely crossed the region, the magistrate would release the prisoners.

Su Lin made an impression on the local women, who would often flee at the sight of her. She worked with the men, collecting plants and small animals, much as Jack had on the Roosevelt expedition. Near the end of the trip—which lasted six months—she shot a brown bear behind the lamasery.

"The lamas told me that was the biggest bear in the whole valley," Quentin Young told me. "They are not happy about it.

57

They think it is a god or something, but I offered them some bear meat and then they forget about it. They hadn't had meat for a long time."

That was not the only thing the Youngs did to annoy the lamas. They witnessed a Tibetan funeral, a "sky burial" in which the lamas dismembered a dead body and left it on a pyre for vultures to eat. Jack and Quentin watched in fascination—then shot one of the vultures, and skinned it, only to be horrified by the stench of death that came out of it.

When they tired of the Minya Konka area, they trekked farther into inner Tibet, ten days west to Litang, which sits on the Tibetan plateau at 14,000 feet. Shortly before they got there, they were met by a horseman, greeting them on behalf of the princess of Kantse, Sikong, and when they arrived in Kantse, the princess herself was waiting for them. She was a young woman about 20, with a broad, sunburned Tibetan face, wearing a black bowler hat, a black satin robe, and a gold medal that had been given to her by the central government in Nanjiang. Her father had ruled two or three counties and called it a kingdom. When he died, his brother took over as regent, and she remained as princess.

She invited the Youngs to her substantial palace, where they drank yak butter tea. The Youngs gave her a flashlight and batteries and other trinkets from the five and ten cent store. She admired their box cameras.

When the Youngs tried to bid her farewell, she insisted they spend the night in the palace, but they refused. They were a little afraid for their safety—Chinese were not well liked in those parts; they could be kidnapped, or worse. But they also didn't want to catch fleas, and the palace was infested.

The princess of Kantse Sikong. Courtesy June Young.

They camped a quarter mile away. In the morning, the princess came to visit their camp with two of her bodyguards, and she invited them back to the palace for a farewell feast of tsampa and yak jerky and wild pears that grew in the region.

The Young brothers continued traveling to the west. They shot snow leopards and golden monkeys in the area around Litang. And with their mission nearly completed, they decided to take a shortcut back to Konka Gompa over a high pass called Djezi La.

One of the guides had suggested the shortcut, because it would save them a day's travel. But it was unmapped, more a rumor than a reality, and it followed a rugged, and at times narrow ridge line that climbed as high as 15,000 feet in altitude. And when the trail petered out, they had to follow the glaciers that fanned down toward the Konka valley.

Late on the second day, a storm blew over them and took whatever patience the altitude had not. Jack, who was always the older brother, was already angry at losing the gamble of the unmarked trail, and he had to worry for the safety of his new wife. And so he sent Quentin ahead to find a place to set up camp for the night.

Quentin was angry at once again being ordered to do the grunt work, but he was relieved to be away from what he perceived as Jack's constant nagging. The sky and the peaks swirled into the blizzard. Quentin's horse broke trail up the pass, struggling through snow up to its chest. At times, the horse foundered in the drifts, and Quentin had to dismount and dig him out. He was as dizzy from the high altitude as from the whiteout, and without the big steady animal between his legs, he might have spun right out into the universe.

An old Kong trapper followed in the gully dug by the horse, impassively carrying a big Tibetan yak hide chest that contained an old Army-style tent, and behind him, an Ullah girl. But there was only so far they could travel in the whiteout, however, and when it grew so severe that Quentin couldn't tell up from down, or moving from standing still, he dismounted, drew his revolver, and fired two warning shots in the air so that Jack would know how far ahead he was. He could barely hear the shots himself for the howling wind and the muffling snow. Instead he wondered at his own judgment for even firing, suddenly remembering the nights he'd lain awake at the lamasery listening to the distant rumbling of avalanches down the peaks and valleys around Minya Konka, places just like where he was standing.

But the altitude did things to your judgment. He remembered once leaving a trail to retrieve something he'd shot, instantly finding himself lost. He'd nearly panicked as he crisscrossed back and forth and finally found the trail.

He and the trapper struggled with the tent while the Ullah girl searched for firewood, hopelessly, because they were high above timberline, and any twigs or branches would have already been buried in the snow.

Jack was suddenly upon them with his wife and the rest of the party, and from the cast of his mouth beneath his dark glasses, Quentin could tell he was even more angry than before.

"Why is there no fire?" he bellowed, even if the answer was obvious.

"Where is the tent?"

"I just got here," Quentin spit back.

They spoke in Cantonese, partly so that Su Lin, who mostly spoke English, would not understand, but she stood by waiting for the explosion she knew was coming.

TOP: *Quentin with Lolo tribesmen and -women. Courtesy Mrs. Vivian Dai.*
BOTTOM: *Camping in Lolo country. Courtesy Mrs. Vivian Dai.*

"How come you just got here?" Jack demanded, and rather than answer, Quentin dramatically threw the tent on the ground.

"I'm not your Ullah girl," he shouted. "This tent can stay in the trunk until you help with it."

Jack turned red.

"Go home, child," he shouted. "I don't need you anymore."

Without thinking, drunk from altitude and exhaustion, Quentin pulled his .38 Colt from its holster. Jack drew his .45, and his voice calmed for the first time.

"Put that away or I'll kill you," Jack whispered.

They stood and glared at each other through the storm's entropy, until Su Lin pushed between them, white with terror, but taking control out of sheer necessity.

"If you kill each other, you'll kill me too," she said.

It was enough to break the stand-off. Without speaking, the two men began to set up the tent. In the morning, the skies had cleared, and they pressed on toward camp. But they didn't speak to each other for two days, and when they did, it was about matters at hand, not about how they had nearly killed each other in a snowbound rage.

Anyway, it was time to head back to civilization. They'd shot several hundred animals, which Jack offered to the American Museum for $300, even though it had cost him more than that to field the expedition. The museum balked at the sum.

But a rare Tibetan white-eared pheasant they'd shot found its way to Mr. F.E. Booth, a San Francisco cannery owner who collected exotic birds on behalf of the California Academy of Sciences. He offered to finance the next year's expedition if the Young brothers would bring such pheasants back to him alive.

* * *

But first, Quentin fell in love. Her name was Tan Eng Tong. She was born in northern China, but her family had migrated to Makassar on the island of Celebes in the Dutch East Indies. She was a tall girl, and at 19, she was two years younger than Quentin. She'd learned Shaolin martial arts from her father and was a bit of a tomboy. So she was an excellent athlete, especially in basketball and track and field. She'd represented her home town in the javelin and discus at the national track competitions, and hoped to make the Chinese team that was training for the 1936 Olympics.

She and Quentin met when the college's men's and women's volleyball teams scrimmaged each other, and their flirting started out as joking. She'd make fun of his slouchy posture, then cover her mouth as she smiled, because she was embarrassed by her own gold tooth. Quentin would comment on her dark complexion. The flirting turned serious when he tagged her out during a softball game, a bit harder than he should have, and that initial anger kindled other passions.

She didn't speak Cantonese, so they would talk to each other in Mandarin or in English. She looked like an Indian, he told her, from Indiana. It was a goofy joke, ignorant of geography, but he carried it further by saying he was going to erase the "In" and call her "Diana." The Chinese spelling of her family name was "Chen," so she became Diana Chen, and she became his goddess of the hunt as well.

Quentin had seriously underestimated how much money he'd need to finish up his degree. He was writing freelance articles to make some cash, but it wasn't enough. Diana, mean-

TOP: *The Youngs traveled up the Yangsi and Min Rivers. Courtesy Mrs. Vivian Dai.*
BOTTOM: *Jack and Su Lin hold a vulture shot at a Tibetan "sky burial."*
Courtesy Mrs. Vivian Dai.

65

A shot of the Konka Gompa lamasery, the staging point for the Minya Konka
trips. Courtesy Mrs. Vivian Dai.

while, had a full scholarship that her wealthy parents were unaware of. She used the money her parents sent to pay Quentin's tuition, which made him very uncomfortable, and all the more anxious to leave school again to follow Jack back to Minya Konka.

In addition to Booth's support, Jack wrote letters to the American Museum and the Bronx Zoo, even mentioning that he'd bring some large traps, and—who knew?—maybe a panda would wander into one of them. The zoo director encouraged him heartily, writing back that if he captured a panda, he'd be able to command a good price for it.

The Young brothers left Shanghai at the end of June, 1935, this time without Su Lin. The Tibetan borderlands were an even more dangerous place than they had been the year before. Just a month earlier, the town of Luding, which they had to pass through, had been the site of a famous battle between the Communists and the Nationalists. The Communists were retreating toward Sichuan in what has come to be known as The Long March. At Luding, the Nationalists had dismantled and booby trapped a chain suspension bridge over the Tung River, and they ambushed the Communists when they reached it. The Communists managed to take the bridge anyway and beat back the Nationalist forces.

So the area was already rife with "bandits," the escaped soldiers of warlord armies, and the armed indigenous tribesmen who didn't much like Chinese traveling through their lands. Now there were also Communist soldiers separated from their units and living off the land.

Jack Young told me of passing caravans of Tibetans armed with blunderbuss rifles that would size them up.

"We had semiautomatic rifles," Jack recalled. "It was no match. All you had to do is fire a few rounds and they run like hell."

Late one night, four or five bandits crept into their camp, armed with swords. Quentin saw a light, then saw one of the intruders and he grabbed a rifle and squeezed off a shot, which woke Jack. Their cook, an ethnic local, called out, "Don't run away. We saw you. We have guns and flashlights and we're going to kill you."

"They could have run away," Quentin said.

Two of them did, and the dog chased them, but the other three froze.

"Why don't you run? I'll shoot you in the eye," Quentin told them.

The brothers tied them head to head and foot to foot, then went back to sleep, leaving the cook to sit up and guard them with a shotgun. In the morning, they marched them to the nearest village and turned them over to the magistrate.

Nonetheless, in Quentin's mind at least, most of the trip was idyllic. He set up a tent in high alpine meadows at 10,000 to 12,000 feet, above a lake, surrounded by snowy peaks, reading the accounts of Chinese and Western explorers and already fantasizing of a day when tour outfitters could bring tourists to that site by helicopter.

As companions he had a dog and an old Lolo trapper named Ren. Ren was about 50; he wore a turban and smoked a long bamboo pipe. He stank of tobacco and yak milk, but they slept in the same tent and shared fleas.

Ren knew how far apart the traps should be, walking them out step by step. The pheasants were creatures of habit.

Each evening, an hour before sundown, they'd fly out of the woods and work their way up the meadow, so skittish that Quentin would not even light a campfire for fear of spooking them.

"When you see those birds gliding down from the other side," he said, "you calculate how long it will be before they reach those traps and you better start, slowly, slowly, and when they are in those traps you run right away. Otherwise they will hurt themselves."

The birds were so wild they would beat themselves to death in the coops they kept behind the lamasery. And when they did, the Youngs would eat them for dinner.

After they had trapped 30 of them, they loaded them into baskets padded with cotton and had coolies pack them part way back to civilization, stashing them beneath the bridge at Luding, with the intention of floating them down the river. They hired a local tribesman to guard the birds until they got back and then hiked back into the mountains to trap 30 more.

But when they returned to Luding, they found that the guard had run away, and the birds had been eaten by bandits, likely Communist stragglers who left behind nothing but bones. As Jack put it, "The Long March came along and they just helped themselves."

Neither brother seemed to remember the urgency with which they hurried out of Sikong and back to Shanghai because Communist forces were converging on Luding. But according to contemporary accounts of the expedition that were published as dispatches in the *China Journal,* they had to abandon some of their equipment to flee the territory before the Communists took over.

THE AMERICAN MUSEUM OF NATURAL HISTORY

has received from

Mr. Jack T. Young Expedition
3 snakes; 9 frogs; 197 mammal
skins with their skulls, including
1 takin, 2 bears, 1 badger, 1 cat
(see over)

*and gratefully acknowledges this
contribution to its collections*

Clarence L. Hay
Secretary

*Seventy-seventh Street and Central Park West
New York, June 24th 1935*

At the end of the trail, a receipt for specimens from the American Museum.
Courtesy Mrs. Vivian Dai.

But they made it back to Shanghai. Of the remaining 30 birds, 19 were still alive when they got there. After days of haggling with customs officials, they were loaded on a freighter headed for San Francisco. Nine survived the crossing only to die after reaching California. Four made it to Booth—one hen and three males—but the hen laid eggs and hatched a brood of pheasants. And by that measure, the expedition was deemed a success!

The trails often meandered along cliff walls . . . Courtesy Mrs. Vivan Dai.

CHAPTER SIX

THE LURE OF
THE GIANT PANDA

The Roosevelt brothers "discovered" the giant panda in that way that English-speaking great men discover everything: by pretending it didn't exist until they set eyes on it. It was an early twentieth century American conceit—in 1911, for example, the American archaeologist Hiram Bingham "discovered" the lost city of Macchu Picchu, when a Peruvian boy led him to it.

Giant Pandas exist in the fossil record, and their historical range covered much of eastern China, even extending as far south as Vietnam and Thailand. It's likely that the emperors who ruled China around the time of Christ's birth, kept pandas in their private zoological gardens.

The animal was first brought to Western attention by a French Jesuit priest named Armand David. Père David had found more success in China as a naturalist than as a missionary, making the Western world aware of several species, such as Père David's deer. While in Sichuan in 1869, he obtained giant panda skins and a skeleton from local hunters which he sent back to the natural history museum in Paris.

David thought he had come across a new species of bear, but a year later, the zoologist Alphonse Milne-Edwards studied the skeleton and determined it was related to the small red panda—thus the name affixed to this newly discovered "giant" version—and consequently was related as well to the raccoon. Indeed there were similarities in the teeth and skulls, and the two pandas shared a diet of bamboo.

The debate whether the two pandas are closely related or whether one is a bear and the other a racoon lingered until DNA studies in the 1980s and -90s showed that the two animals were not so closely related after all.

Though bears and racoons do indeed have common ancestors, the red panda crept out on its own evolutionary branch from the raccoon side of the family. The giant panda, on the other hand, lumbered away from the bear family some 20 million years ago.

George Schaller is Director for Science of The Wildlife Conservation Society and one of the wildlife biologists who helped set up the Chinese government's panda studies. When asked whether giant pandas are bears or raccoons, Schaller likes to say, "The panda is a panda," as solitary in its zoological peculiarity as it is solitary in the wild.

It grows to five or six feet long and weighs between 150 and 275 pounds, and its anatomy is similar to most species of bears, except that its teeth and jaws, and to a lesser extent, its digestive tract, have adapted to its bamboo diet.

Bears are omnivores; they eat meat and fish when they can get it, and when they can't, they eat nuts and berries and grass. Judging from their digestive tracts, so should giant pandas. But alas, they are not fast enough or clever enough to catch those creatures that live in their mountainous lair, and so they eat bamboo instead. In fact they eat practically nothing but bamboo, and in prodigious quantities: 20 to 30 pounds a day, even more at certain times of year. But since their gut is not equipped to process bamboo, most of it passes through them undigested. The giant panda only absorbs an average of 17 percent of the bamboo it eats, and so it must eat constantly, and when not feeding, conserve precious energy.

At present, its habitat is split into six mountainous regions covering about 5,400 square miles in Sichuan, Gansu and Shaanxi, along the eastern edge of the Tibetan plateau. Given the elusive nature of the animal and the remoteness of its territory, it's no wonder that none were seen by Westerners in the 60 years after David's discovery. There were a few unconfirmed sightings by explorers passing through Tibet, pandas they thought they spotted in trees or at a distance, but no certainties.

The Roosevelts, however, were *not* the first Westerners to see a live panda. In 1914, a German naturalist named Dr. Hugo Weigold bought four giant panda skins and a live giant panda cub from hunters in Sichuan. He had intended to bring the cub back alive to Europe, but it died, and so he had it skinned and brought it back with the other carcasses. But this information was soon overshadowed by the First World War, and Americans were obviously not going to pay much attention to what a German expedition had done.

So when they left China with their panda in 1929, the Roosevelts—and the entire English-speaking zoological establishment, for that matter—believed that they had achieved a first. They were certainly the first Westerners to *shoot* the animal, a distinction that seems a lot less noble from a twenty-first century perspective.

(Certainly the Roosevelts had no hesitations about editing history. One of the Roosevelt associates on the Indochina leg of their Field expedition had contracted malaria and died while in a hospital in Vientiane. The first letters back to the States said that he'd died of a "violent cerebral attack." Perhaps he did, after a fashion: documents I found in the Field archives revealed that, in fact, he'd thrown himself from a high hospital window while in a feverish delirium. But apparently such things were not talked of openly.)

The second Westerner to shoot a giant panda was Ernst Schaefer, a German on a 1931 American expedition led by Brooke Dolan on behalf of the Philadelphia Academy of Sciences. Schaefer spotted a six-month-old panda cub in a tree, and though he probably could have captured it, he shot it instead. (Later, in 1935, a second Brooke Dolan expedition crossed paths with Jack and Quentin Young's second trip to Minya Konka. Quentin Young has a photograph of himself and Schaefer seated in the courtyard of a Lolo village.)

And subsequently, other Great White Hunters came to China to do the same. They were a close-knit fraternity—they knew each other in New York and they corresponded with each other when they were in the field.

The chronicler of their expeditions to China was Arthur de Carle Sowerby, the Chinese-born child of English missionaries. He was an explorer and a naturalist in his own right, and he founded the *China Journal*, a Shanghai-based monthly that interpreted everything about China—history, anthropology, science, current events—to English speakers. Su Lin Young, Jack Young's wife, was an editorial staffer there in the mid-1930s when these hunts took place. Every month in a column headlined "Expedition Notes" and written by Sowerby, real and

Dean Sage and his wife make camp in panda country near Zhaopo.
Courtesy China Journal.

would-be sportsmen alike could read that the Brooke Dolan Expedition was nearing Tibet or that the Youngs' Sikong Expedition was fleeing the rapidly advancing Communist forces.

Another rich New York Ivy Leaguer named Dean Sage was the next sportsman to proudly shoot a giant panda. He did so late in 1934, and of course he published his exclusive first-person account of the kill in *China Journal* just months later.

Sage was trailing what he thought were old panda tracks through snow and bamboo thickets in the Zhaopo Valley, when the native hunters and their dogs started a giant panda from its lair. In its confusion, the big animal charged straight at Sage, and Sage unloaded the chamber of his rifle into the panda's chest without dropping it. Then he heard hollow clicks as his gun dry fired. He was out of ammunition and thought for an instant that he was going to have to club the still-charging panda

Sage's panda, the second killed by Great White Hunters. Courtesy China Journal.

with his rifle butt. But fortunately, an alert porter pressed another cartridge into his hand, which he loaded and shot.

At the same time, a companion named William Sheldon fired on the panda from above on the hill (and so did a number of the native hunters, but Sage discounted the possibility they could have actually hit his panda), and the animal finally fell dead. Sage skinned it and then packed the viscera in formaldehyde to ship back to the American Museum in New York to be studied by scientists there. And though Jack Young had already provided a panda pelt to the museum, this was treated as the museum's first.

Next, according to Sowerby, another European, one Captain H.C. Brockelhurst, who had been a game warden in the Sudan, shot another panda the next year.

In February, 1935, the very same volume of *China Journal* that featured Sage's dramatic adventure, ran an item in the Expedition Notes under the headline "The Lure of the Giant Panda."

One Mr. W.H. Harkness, Jr., it reported, had come to China with a couple of hearty companions to capture pandas alive. The article concluded that "it would appear as though they had a good chance of being successful, at least as far as securing live specimens of this remarkable animal is concerned."

Bill Harkness was a small man with slicked-back blond hair and a clipped little mustache like the one Adolph Hitler wore. He was in his early 30s, a Harvard man, which was an important credential in those days; it canceled out the fact that he had no real profession to speak of. What he did have was enough family money to finance his adventures.

With all the gallantry of the 1930s, he was posthumously described as an all-American boy, "game to the core," a "straight-shooter." But the truth is, he was impulsive and somewhat irresponsible. The newspapers referred to Harkness as a "youthful amateur zoologist" and an "adventurer scientist." At Harvard, he'd studied ethnology, which is an offshoot of anthropology. Before reaching China, his panda expedition had stopped in the Philippines to undertake an anthropological study.

But he was not a "sportsman" like the Roosevelts. He was a "bring-'em-back-alive" hunter. While it might have been glamorous to have a museum finance one's extended hunting vacation to exotic lands under pretense of "collecting," it was even more impressive to bring the animals back alive for everyone to see. And it marked a transition in the study of zoology, from examining the carcasses of dead animals to studying them alive—even if it stopped short of studying them in their habitats, which in the 1930s might have been a prohibitively difficult task.

Fortunately, there were brash young adventurers like Bill Harkness willing to risk their lives to capture dangerous and exotic beasts. The reward was a moment's notoriety, sort of a peacetime medal of bravery. He'd done it before. In 1934, Harkness and a partner named Lawrence Griswold traveled to the Malaysian island of Komodo to capture Komodo lizards. Griswold was an archaeologist who'd graduated Harvard two years before Harkness, a tall, dark, serious-looking fellow with a professorial van Dyke beard.

Using box traps baited with pig and deer entrails, they captured 13 of the lizards in eight days, released five because they were less than seven feet long, and wrestled eight back to civilization. The Malaysian government forced them to turn half of them over to the national agricultural department, which repaid them by quarantining Harkness and Griswold's specimens and then rushing the other four to the United States to see if they could corner the zoo market before the two Americans could sell theirs.

The lizards were truly fierce creatures that would fling themselves against the sides of their cages trying to get at the humans beyond. But at the same time they were rather fragile, at risk of tearing themselves apart in their own fury. Harkness and Griswold kept theirs in a Singapore zoo while they waited for the winter weather in New York to warm to more lizard-friendly temperatures. They arrived in Vancouver in May, 1934, with three animals still alive, and sold one to the National Zoo in Washington for $500 and the other two to the Bronx Zoo for $700. All of the reptiles died of intestinal infection within a year.

Lawrence Griswold (left) and William H. Harkness, Jr., before they embarked on their panda hunt. Courtesy New York Times *Pictures.*

Harkness and Griswold called themselves the first hunters to capture the dragons. Letters to the *New York Times* from careful readers pointed to others already in captivity, but no matter. It was still an impressive credential.

Nonetheless, Harkness was not part of the close-knit society of Great White Hunters. In August of 1934, when Dean Sage was on his way to shoot his panda, he posted a letter from Shanghai to C.D. Carter, curator at the American Museum in New York, to pass on some gossip.

He wrote about the usual suspects: "Dolan went up four or five weeks ago," he wrote. "Jack Young is on his way out," and so on. And near the end of the letter he posed a somewhat cynical question:

"My mother-in-law sent us a clipping from the *Sun* about a mammoth expedition that was coming out here soon under the leadership of a fellow called Harkness," he wrote. "Their modest ambition seems to be to capture eight Giant Panda alive. I wonder if you saw the clipping, and also what museum Harkness is going for. I know him slightly."

The phrase "modest ambition" seems to imply that Sage didn't think Harkness had a chance. Carter was on a collecting vacation himself when the letter arrived and didn't respond until November. By then, Harkness was already en route.

"You speak of an expedition under the leadership of Harkness," Carter wrote. "He and his sidekick came in to see me sometime in August, I believe, and told me they hoped to organize an expedition to bring out giant panda alive. I do not recall that he said any specific number or that he hoped to get as many as eight. They had brought back specimens of the Komodo Island lizard and seemed to be fairly reasonable in their plans and expectations."

The next sentence posed a sneering question of its own, based on the exaggerated drama of those hunters who actually *had* shot pandas.

"Whether one can really bring out giant panda alive, of course, is a questionable matter," Carter wrote, "and probably the Press has played up the expedition on extravagant terms."

Could anyone really capture an animal alleged to be so fierce? Harkness was so sure he could, that he had already shopped around for zoos willing to buy his potential pandas. The Bronx Zoo did not offer funding up front, but its director assured Harkness that if he managed to secure such an animal, the zoo would happily pay the cost of shipping it to New York.

Harkness set sail on September 22, 1934, with four companions, including Griswold. In some accounts, Griswold is listed as the expedition's leader and senior scientist. Two weeks before, Harkness had married a longtime friend, Ruth McCombs. As the expedition embarked from New York, she described his companions as "four of the biggest men I have ever seen—ranging from six feet to six-feet-five, Bill bringing up the rear rather like a terrier in the wake of great Danes."

They traveled first to the Philippines to do "anthropological" work, but instead found the kind of adventure that makes for good newspaper stories. They'd hired a launch to take them from the Philippines to Borneo, but it broke down within sight of land and drifted out toward the open waters of the Celebes Sea, a region known for its merciless pirates. They were adrift for four days before they managed to repair the engine.

In a letter published in the *New York Times*, Griswold described an oncoming storm (a dropping barometer at least). They'd had to ration water, but as Griswold tells it, some Chinese passengers became hysterical and had to be held at gun point for the greater safety of the Griswold-Harkness Expedition.

In her book, Ruth Harkness jauntily describes this as "a near ship-wreck in the Celebes Sea, and a forced landing at Tawao on Borneo in time for Christmas dinner—adventures all royally played up by the press, and exciting enough, but not exactly conducive to the peace of mind of the stay-at-home wife."

Sowerby refers to their "misadventures" in his writing about Bill Harkness, but refuses to go into any detail, almost as if they were too sordid to discuss. They may have been: Three of the expeditionaries, including Lawrence Griswold, decided to scuttle the panda hunt altogether. They dropped out before they left the Philippines, leaving Harkness and Griswold's cousin, Le Grand Griswold to carry on.

The survivors reached Shanghai in January, 1935—and got nowhere fast. They'd tried to go through the necessary governmental channels, but could not obtain permits to travel to the interior because of Communist activity there. It did not help, one supposes, that they were not part of the usual club of foreign hunters. And according to an English associate named Gerald Russell, Chinese officials were not amused by the Harkness-Griswold Expedition's escapades in the Phillippines, especially as it related to Chinese nationals.

By July, Harkness was the only original member of the expedition who hadn't given up and gone home. *China Journal*'s Expedition Notes politely explained that LeGrand Griswold had returned to the United States on urgent family business and that Harkness was being joined by Russell, and a "veteran West China explorer" named Floyd Tangier Smith.

Floyd Smith came from an important Long Island family, though he hardly ever lived on Long Island. He was born in 1882, in Japan, where his parents were missionaries. He went to military school in Ohio, and then attended Dartmouth University and Bowdoin College. By 1908, he was trying to make a respectable career for himself as a banker, but it bored him, so he found a job with the American Trading Company in New York, got himself transferred to India and then to Shanghai. And while in Shanghai, he quit the daily working life altogether and became a hunter and an explorer. With the passage of years he became what was glamorously referred to as an "Old China Hand."

Smith had short hair and a long gaunt face set off by wire-rimmed spectacles. To make up for his less-than-dashing appearance, he had an outsized ego. He called himself "Ajax." He bragged of his many adventures, the horses he'd owned, the bandits he'd defeated, the important people he knew. His long-winded letters to museum curators also claimed that he, Smith, was the only Anglo in China who was capable of navigating the boggling Chinese bureaucracy. But he apparently was able to do so with great charm.

Ruth Harkness later described a character she called "Zoology Jones"—who was obviously Smith—as "a boy of fifty-five or sixty, [he was 54] a soldier of fortune, with adventure and success always just around the corner."

Quentin Young disliked Smith without ever meeting him, because he thought that Smith was English, and he hated the English. Smith had a cook and a house boy, like many foreigners in China. In Young's opinion, that clinched it: Smith was a typical overbearing rich white man in China, and Quentin Young resented him. Besides, Young told me, "He thinks he is the king of that place," referring to Smith's territorial claims over several remote Chinese hunting grounds.

Jack Young was more forgiving of Smith's character.

"He had to maintain the white man's prestige," Jack Young told me by way of explaining Smith's pretentious lifestyle. "Oh, he was a very congenial fellow," Jack Young continued, "you know, well read for his profession. But he was a rough-and-ready type who would not take no for an answer."

Gerald Russell apparently liked him enormously, and in a 1965 letter, described Smith as "the cream of the earth, a great gentleman, esteemed and loved by all. He seemed to have been a journalist most of his life, and was considered the greatest expert on banditry in China. But animals were his love; consequently he lived precariously."

Smith started collecting full time for the Field Museum in 1930. While other Great White Hunters came as tourists from New York and Philadelphia, Smith was permanently stationed in Shanghai and making a good living—at least until the Great Depression caught up to his managers at the Field Museum.

He'd received mostly high praise from the Field for the quality of specimens he sent to Chicago, but nonetheless, the Field took him off the payroll in mid-1932, forcing him to freelance like Jack Young. At the end of the letter bearing this bad news, the Field curator wrote, "I regret the necessity of bringing the work to a close, but if you have been at all in touch with world affairs during this past year, probably you will not be surprised."

Smith, in fact, was aware of all kinds of Chinese surprises that the Field curator couldn't imagine. His letters to his clients in Chicago and elsewhere describe the soap opera of his life. Though he lived in China, he had a strong disdain for the Chinese. He always blamed his worthless Chinese assistants for anything that went wrong with his collecting. He accused them of criminal neglect. He ranted about customs officials who dared open the containers he tried to ship abroad, about one middle-aged camp assistant who ruined his plans by running off with a local teenage girl.

The Chinese returned his contempt. Smith was frequently at odds with local warlords and Bolshevik students upriver in Sichuan, which was a hotbed for Communist activity. One of his camps was burned to the ground, one of his employees shot to death. His permits were yanked. But he kept multiple camps in various remote areas, from Chengdu up to Zhaopo, each of them staffed with Chinese assistants, and he hired cadres of local hunters and trappers who did the actual collecting.

"The mountaineers are very primitive, superstitious, unenterprising, stupid and ultra conservative," he later wrote to Sowerby, "and it took months of strenuous missionary work, and the expenditure of many thousands of dollars, to get the new idea of profit in live animals in their heads. I plastered the whole valley [. . .] and sent out men all over the country advertising that all post offices would pay cash for live birds and animals."

In effect, he established collecting centers, where his hunters—that is to say *any* hunters—could bring the animals they shot or trapped or captured alive.

In one letter to the Field, he mentioned the possibility that he'd lend some of his men to a hunter named Jack Young, apparently unaware that the Field had trained Young years before.

On paper, Smith was a great and magnanimous man. He was also quite a liar. Jack Young claimed Smith rarely went into the field himself, and that the "trappers" were not so much Smith's faithful employees, or even hunters, for that matter, but herb diggers who would sign on to work for whoever came through. But certainly, the scale of Smith's operation made him a conspicuous target for Chinese officials. This, after all, was an era in which the Chinese were more than tired of arrogant Westerners earning a living off of their own national treasures.

Smith brought out quite a few of those treasures. Late in 1932, even though he was no longer a salaried employee of the Field, he delivered more than 1,400 mammal specimens to that institution, including a giant panda skin and seven takins, which are large horned creatures that look like a cross between a horse and a goat. He'd delivered two live red pandas to San Francisco—the "wildcats" that Jack Young's mountaineering companions described when they met Smith on their voyage up the Yangsi—and this was a minor coup.

Despite his congenial nature and his good reputation, his long confessional letters reveal a depressed and troubled man with more than his share of health problems.

Over the course of several letters to President Simms at the Field Museum, he describes his infected teeth, his tuberculosis, a couple of hemorrhoid operations that led to a "distressing bowel complaint," double pneumonia, the "beginnings of a heart problem" that kept him from going to high altitudes, and "nerve fag due to the continued difficulties faced in attempting to do too big a job without enough money."

Under the grandiose exterior, he was losing his composure. He had been unable to secure a complete giant panda carcass for the Field Museum to match the one Sage had secured for the American Museum. He was trying to capture live pheasants for a private collector in California, a Pasadena scion named Keith Spalding. In June, 1935, when he had run out of money, he cabled Spalding and asked for more, and was turned down flat. But he'd seized on one more possibility, one big score, as he wrote in yet another letter to the Field.

"The changed plans for another trip have come about through the opportunity to act as general manager and guide to a party who desired to make a trip into the same country, but were not able to handle it or even secure permits to make a start alone," he wrote.

It was the Harkness panda expedition. Bill Harkness held promise of Smith's salvation. But Smith had no idea how many new problems Harkness would cause.

Gossip travels quickly, even over oceans. Before he headed up toward Minya Konka to capture pheasants with his brother, Jack Young dashed off a letter to Dr. Carter at the American Museum to share news of the Harkness expedition. Young had met

Harkness in New York right after he returned from the Dutch East Indies with the Komodo lizards. Now Young was reporting on Harkness's escapades in Shanghai.

"Remember Harkness and Griswold?" he wrote. "Well, the Chinese authority refused them permission, and for a while Harkness disappeared completely—even Griswold couldn't find him and no reason accounted for. The American Consulate got all hot and bothered. Finally, after three weeks of searching, they, with the help of the [international] settlement detective force, located him in the Palace Hotel registered under an assumed name. Before his discovery, news of his disappearance reached Harkness' wife in New York. She thought he was kidnapped by the Chinese bandits! She went to the State Department—so the story goes—to demand them to protest to the Chinese Government. While all these were going on, Harkness was probably polishing the waxed floor at some local joint with some blonde Russian girl friend. Anyway, he told Consul Cunningham that since permission for his expedition was refused, he wants to enjoy life and doesn't want to be bothered—so he couldn't understand all the fuss to locate him. Just now, FT Smith and he are joining up and plan to go up river after the dozen of live Giant Pandas together. What next—Heaven knows!"

Carter quickly relayed the information in a note to his friend Dean Sage. Carter didn't think Smith should even get involved with an upstart like Harkness, and he let Sage know. Then he wrote a polite response to Jack Young, saying as much:

"I was interested to hear what you had to say about Harkness. I saw about some of his doings in the New York papers. I should not think it would be well for Smith's prestige to be connected with him."

The tale of Harkness going AWOL had already leaked out and appeared in a two-inch story buried deep inside the *New York Times*. Harkness had been missing for two weeks, and when the police found him, they dragged him before the district attorney, who ordered him to report to his office every three days.

Harkness told the *Times* that he would soon be returning to New York. It had been a hard several months for him. In addition to his Chinese misfortunes and misadventures, his father, a retired New York lawyer, had been killed in an automobile accident in Holbrook, Arizona. He was undergoing quite a few emotional trials, but his companions had put up with enough.

"I am as mystified as any one at his strange behavior," Le Grand Griswold told the *Times*. "This puts an end to our panda hunting expedition, and I am returning to America at the first opportunity."

Griswold politely told the Shanghai press, including The *China Journal*, that he had been called back to the U.S. "on urgent family affairs."

Smith was increasingly alarmed, but he kept his opinion of Harkess's peculiar behavior to himself, because he needed Harkness's money. He even covered up for him in letters to the Field curators, saying that Harkness had not been "dissipating" but had been holed up in hotels reading books. Apparently the news leaked out anyway, because, as Smith wrote, " . . . a good deal of unfavorable comment had appeared in the press and it was even suggested that he should be sent home as being of unsound mind."

Harkness wanted to hunt pandas. Smith had a laundry list of creatures he owed to the Field and to Spalding. Harkness had money. Smith had a field camp set up in the Zhaopo Valley, and though Sage and Brockelhurst had shot their pandas in that area, Smith "thought he was king of that place," as Quentin Young said.

But he couldn't even get to his own kingdom. Smith and Harkness and Russell were turned back because of battles between the Nationalists and the Communists, and so they cooled their heels in Chonqing through a searingly hot summer, waiting until Sichuan was reclaimed from the Communists.

Smith's problems only worsened. His men had captured more than 100 pheasants, he told Spalding, which were eaten by Communist soldiers—as had happened to some of the pheasants captured by the Young brothers. Then Russell got tired and dropped out of the expedition. In late September, Smith and Harkness returned to Shanghai because the Chinese government had accused them of not having the proper permits, according to a *China Journal* note, headlined "Harkness and Smith Return." Smith denied the charge, to little avail.

By then, Harkness had developed a painful swelling in his neck. He saw a doctor in Shanghai and had surgery to remove the growth.

On October 13, Smith traveled to the capital at Nanjiang and finally wrested permits from the authorities for the trip upriver. When he got back to Shanghai, however, he found that Harkness was gone again. Rather than report back to the hospital for more surgery, instead he'd taken off on another bender. The doctor was most concerned, because he had not yet told Harkness that the growth he removed was malignant. Harkness had cancer, and if the doctor didn't remove more tissue within weeks, Harkness could die.

Smith alerted the proper authorities, and great hunter that he was, he staked out Harkness's bank, figuring he'd have to come out of his lair sooner or later to get money. Five weeks after the disappearance, Smith caught him there and bundled him off to the hospital.

To add insult to injury, at about the same time, Jack and Quentin Young had returned to Shanghai with a brace of live pheasants that they were shipping to California. Smith, "the king of that place" churned out a long letter to Spalding.

"And another bitter pill to swallow at this time is the circumstance that Jack T. Young, the man I trusted and financed to get the white birds from Tatsienlu, very joyfully took the money," he wrote, "succeeded in collecting 24 birds all winter . . . succeeded in getting two to America, for his own account, on my (or rather your) money. But those two were picked up by Mr. F.E. Booth of San Francisco, who immediately thereafter financed Jack Young to go back for more.

"I am not concerned at all over the possibility of his being able to make anything of a success of this sporadic venture since all he knows is what I taught him (and I gave him the best that I could out of 15 years of my trial and error experience) after which his best efforts over a whole winter, in a place where birds are thick, amounted to no more than two delivered. Which two, incidentally, belong to me (by rights) or, rather, to Mrs. Spalding.

"But what does concern me in this is the whole sentiment of the present Chinese official regime in 'all things Chinese for the Chinese only' and since Jack Young is an American born Cantonese, I am not at all sure that he may not be able to pull official strings to effect a cancellation of the permit to export that I had secured [and which Smith thought would be the last issued], so that if he cannot succeed I at least may not be permitted to do so."

Fifty-five years into the future, when I showed this letter to Jack Young, his mouth dropped open, because he only knew Smith socially and had never worked for him, and certainly hadn't been trained by him.

Smith soon had more bitter pills to swallow. Harkness was released from the hospital on Christmas Day and seemed to be on the road to recovery. Then after a few weeks he began to rapidly lose weight. In January, 1936, the doctor discovered that the cancer had spread to Harkness's colon, and initially wanted to treat it with X-rays. But it worsened too quickly. Harkness went into the hospital for emergency surgery on January 18, 1936, and died on the operating table at around four the next morning. He was 33.

Twelve hours later, a phone call reached his wife's apartment in New York while she was out getting a shampoo. When Ruth Harkness returned home, she was hit with the bad news. Bill Harkness had never even told her he was ill, and she didn't know what killed him until she got to China. And she never even revealed the malady in interviews or in her own writing, touching off speculation that her husband had died of venereal disease or gunshot wounds or perished in some other "unseemly" manner. Perhaps that wasn't far from the truth: many at the time believed cancer stemmed from lack of cleanliness; it was certainly not mentioned in polite company.

In another hour or so, Ruth Harkness received a telegram from Secretary of State Cordell Hull, confirming the death. Hull informed her that her husband had more than $1,500 in a bank account in Shanghai. He also noted that undertakers in Shanghai were standing by and could ship the body home in a sealed casket for $850 or cremate it and ship the ashes back in a copper urn for $100. She chose cremation and had her lawyers return instructions to transfer the money to her in New York.

Floyd Smith assumed he'd carry on his expedition with the money Harkness left, and said so in one of his letters. He wrote, "... according to Harkness's expressed wish, the expedition will be carried through as far as remaining funds, already allocated, may permit, with his wife in his place as far as concerns his share in any financial benefit that may result."

Smith was willing to pay a reasonable return to Ruth Harkness on what was gained with her husband's money. But Smith never thought that Ruth Harkness would actually show up in China and want to take part herself. The stress of it all put him back in the hospital, though this time he thought he was suffering a relapse of malaria. And even when Ruth Harkness showed up at his door, he was thinking more about using Bill's money for his own collecting needs and not for the futile effort of chasing live pandas.

In a letter to the Field Museum in October, 1936, he wrote, "Plans at the moment are completely at loose ends as the widow of Mr. Harkness, who wished me to carry on with the original expedition, had ideas that were completely impractical from my point of view (and from hers too if she did but know it) and any continuance of that activity had to be abandoned, leaving me to change horses in the middle of the stream with no provision made ahead of time for remounts."

CHAPTER SEVEN

RUTH

Ruth Harkness's decision to sail for China and take off after giant pandas was one of those desperate and misinformed decisions that sometimes lead to great things. She was chasing a husband she barely knew, bored with her life, more anxious, perhaps, to find *herself* than some exotic and ill-evolved mammal that lived near Tibet. She knew no more about animals than the average New York urbanite, and she bragged that she was in no physical shape to trek two thousand miles into the wild.

When her husband-to-be, Bill Harkness, had told her he was going to China to capture a giant "pandar," Ruth, no student of zoology, corrected him.

"You mean giant *panther,* don't you?" she asked.

He meant "panda," and what he—like most anyone, for that matter—knew about them he'd learned by reading the Roosevelts' book, *Trailing the Giant Panda.*

"Knowledge of the panda was practically non-existent," Ruth wrote in her 1938 book, *The Lady and the Panda,* "and the attempt to capture one alive was a shot in the dark—one chance in million, but, he thought, and so did I, well worth the risk."

Ruth Harkness mugging with Su Lin. © The Chicago Tribune.

Such was the common wisdom. There was nothing common about Ruth Harkness, however. She was diminutive in stature—just five feet, four inches tall—but she was large in affect. Her nieces called her "dashing Aunt Ruth." She had dark hair that she never cut and instead wound around her head or wrapped in a turban. Occasionally she'd let it down and wrap herself in a blanket to prove how much she looked like an Indian and thus convince people of her one-thirty-second Cherokee blood.

She was hardly a beauty by any aesthetic. She had a long and rather pinched face, but she had a manner about her, an eye for clothes, for the right facial expression, and the right words to talk her way out of trouble. After an hour with her—and probably a Manhattan or two—one would find her charming and attractive indeed.

She was born Ruth McCombs, the daughter of a carpenter, in the little town of Titusville, in western Pennsylvania, a town that had been founded by her great-great-something grandfather after the Revolutionary War. That ancestor had allegedly bought it from Native Americans, she would say, calling on hazy family memories, and one of the family had married into the tribe, which is why she could claim Indian blood. In a bio she later typed out for her literary agent, she wrote that her Indian ancestry, "Possibly accounts for ability to get along beautifully with Chinese or any Orientals, including Peruvian Indians."

To her advantage, Ruth McCombs Harkness was a scandal wherever she went. The conservative denizens of Titusville, for example, had been alarmed by her penchant for skinny-dipping in a local creek, even though she couldn't swim very well. Which is to say she was more daring than sensible.

Her younger sister Harriet (who has since passed away) told me, "When she got in trouble, she could look so helpless— she wasn't helpless at all—but she could get people to help her that way."

After high school, she found a factory job in Erie to make and save money for college. Then she tried to attend the University of Colorado, but found its sorority system to be small-minded, and didn't even last out her first year. So she fled to the wide-open city of Havana, ostensibly to teach English. And when she'd worn herself out there, the next logical stop on the libertine highway was New York, where she landed in 1925, at the age of 24.

"She was a little country girl from Titusville, but she became a really sophisticated New Yorker," said her niece, Jane

Jones (who also has passed away). "She was more sophisticated than anybody I ever knew. She could hold people spellbound just talking. She was not a real beauty, but she had a terrific flair for wearing clothes—dramatically, too."

That flair was her livelihood in New York. She worked as a stylist, fashion consultant, and buyer for various Fifth Avenue shops, until the Depression left her unemployed in 1929. So she moved in with her brother and his family, followed them from Trenton, New Jersey, to Jamaica, Queens, and taught herself how to design clothing. She had a bit of a fashion coup when she reintroduced cotton calico as the fabric for a little housecoat that she sold to a catalog house.

On September 9, 1934, on a lark, she married Bill Harkness. She'd known him for about ten years, although they hadn't really courted. Bill Harkness had just returned from the Dutch East Indies with his "dragons," which obviously fascinated Ruth McCombs.

"There were long evenings spent in talk of adventure and exploration—of the little-known corners of the earth," she later wrote. "We had been doing just that for years and exchanging books that dealt with travel and adventure."

Perhaps she was latching on to his notoriety, his adventuresome personality, or both.

"I don't think there was anything romantic about it," Jane Jones said. She thought her aunt was one of the few people who actually got to know Bill Harkness.

"She probably took him seriously," Jones told me. "She really believed in his efforts to find a panda."

And perhaps they were drinking buddies. Jones admitted a family secret that Bill Harkness had a penchant for disappearing on alcoholic binges even before his eye-catching escapades in Shanghai. And she admitted that Ruth drank hard as well.

But marriage wouldn't have been a big priority in Ruth Harkness's world view. Jones recalled that when a family friend gave up her profession to become a housewife, dashing Aunt Ruth was "a-*ghast*!" And if the family was shocked that Ruth wed, they were not surprised in the manner she chose to do so, unannounced, at the city clerk's office.

"Just what I would expect of her," Jones said.

Ruth Harkness described her own surprise.

"In September of 1934 Bill and I discovered that we were no longer just the good friends that we had been for ten years, and in the last-minute rush of expedition affairs we found the time to be married," she wrote.

Whether or not they were really suited for each other was never tested, because they never lived together. Perhaps she thought that if she married him, he'd have to take her along on his forthcoming adventure, but he made it clear to her, in no uncertain terms, that there was no room for a woman on such a dangerous and manly expedition. He did lead her to believe that she might be able to join him later.

Thirteen days after the wedding, he was on his way to the Philippines. Ruth Harkness passed time with her brother on a trip to the Virgin Islands, then settled into an apartment in Manhattan with a couple of friends.

Bill Harkness's letters home were filled with accounts of his adventures and misadventures, of his troubles with the Chinese authorities. Ruth expected to join him when he was settled. But he put off the time when she'd be able to visit with him in China, and dismissed it as altogether impractical when he wrote to tell her he'd finally received government permission to go "upriver."

He never let on that he was ill, so it was doubly shocking for her to learn he was dead in Shanghai when she thought he'd already left for the interior. She claimed that she never learned what killed him until she reached China herself, several months later.

Two months after his death, she was on her way. She told the *New York Times*, "I inherited an expedition, and what else could I do?" Her reasons were likely not so simplistic. Gerald Russell, her husband's English partner, later claimed that he'd seen Ruth Harkness in New York shortly after Bill's death and suggested to her that since "she owned so much equipment along the Yangtse [Yangsi] and in Shanghai, she should continue the expedition her husband had started."

Quentin Young felt she came to China out of longing and anger. She wanted to experience everything her husband had experienced—and had denied her. Young felt she was angry in that way of a wife whose husband goes off and dies and leaves her to fend for herself, while in the process killing a lifetime of her dreams. Angry, perhaps, that he'd never even warned her he was sick, and perhaps angry at his embarrassingly foolish behavior in Shanghai. Jack Young, in his letter to a curator in New York, mentioned that Ruth Harkness had called on the State Department to find her husband the first time he'd disappeared. She worried that he been kidnapped by bandits on the trail, only to discover he'd been on a bender at the Palace Hotel in Shanghai.

If Ruth Harkness's family had been surprised when she married, they were not the least bit surprised when she set sail for China on April 17, 1936, and they all turned out to see her off in grand style. Harkness's book, *The Lady and the Panda*, is a delightful account of that trip, written in the unmistakable style of 1930s travel writing, jaunty, unsinkable, in a tone of voice that implies the author is happily sauntering along with one hand in a pants pocket, a cigarette dangling from the lips, and a cynical twinkle in the eye.

Gerald Russell claimed that Harkness crossed Europe by train. She picked up her narrative on board ship through the Suez Canal. As she made port in Aden, Ceylon, and Manila, she wrote of her growing excitement, and she was absolutely fascinated with China from the first hours that the ship was threading its way through islands into Hong Kong's harbor.

She wrote effusively of the junks in the harbors, and she ascribed mystic qualities to the Chinese she met or even just saw from afar. The "boys" in the hotel seemed to know exactly what she wanted without being able to speak to her in any mutually intelligible language, the ricksha drivers seemed to know where she wanted to go without speaking.

She found Shanghai less attractive than Hong Kong (which is surprising, because Shanghai in the 1930s was another of those wide-open cities where Westerners could live large without having to answer to local authorities—in other words, it was her kind of town), and she checked into the Palace Hotel, because she remembered that Bill had stayed there once. In fact that was where the authorities found him after he disappeared.

For her first couple of weeks in Shanghai, she worked at tidying up Bill's affairs, which included meetings with Russell and his and Bill's recent partner, Mr. Floyd Tangier Smith. Though Harkness never so much as mentioned his name in her book, Smith later reiterated that Russell, in effect, was acting as her business manager in Shanghai.

There are a number of things that Harkness fictionalized in her book, including Smith's name. She probably did so to avoid libel. After all, by the time her book came out, Smith had already accused her of fraud and theft, all in his tediously bombastic style. That she gave him the pseudonym "Zoology Jones," is delightfully prescient of Steven Spielberg's film character, Indiana Jones, another purported adventurer-scientist from the same era.

Even if Smith's letters to the Field Museum were long laments about his health and financial problems, not to mention the "nerve fag" that Bill Harkness and Jack Young had caused him, he was putting on a good front for Mrs. Harkness, if she did but know it (as he might have said). He dazzled her with his great knowledge—when all she wanted was the straight dope on her husband.

"There was all the tangle of their accounts to straighten out (and they never really were cleared up);" she wrote, "the lists of equipment to go over, and that was a job because it was scattered from Shanghai to Chengtu. It was also a job that was hard to stick to, because it was always much more interesting to listen to Zoology's tales of hunting in far Western China in the high hills, the animals to be found in those snow-capped mountains—animals that live nowhere else in the world. There were the tales of the Panchen Lama, civil war, bandits, the race horses Zoology owned and gold in the high hills."

Harkness wrote that she would frequently dine with Smith and his wife (who was half-Japanese) in Japanese restaurants, though there are suggestions in the record that some of those conversations took place in Smith's hospital room. Regardless, Smith still clung to his belief that there was no sense limiting the hunt to live pandas, since it was such hard goal to attain and since there was guaranteed profit and glory in other species. Harkness was not convinced.

"It somehow didn't interest me," she wrote. "I wouldn't have known a tragopan from a tufted deer..."

Smith then tried to scare her off traveling upriver by spinning dramatic yarns about bandits and bureaucratic red tape, about dysentery and bad weather and the difficult terrain. But none of those hardships impressed her either.

Smith still could not get permits to travel upriver, apparently, and Russell claimed that he encouraged Harkness to go by herself, without a permit. Unsure exactly what to do, Harkness flew to Beijing to make some effort of warning the American consul that she intended to go panda hunting, even if she didn't yet know how.

The consul was extremely condescending to her, "practically shaking a finger under my nose," she wrote, and she claimed he said, "Now don't you go running around China antagonizing people as some of our American 'explorers' do or you'll get into all kinds of trouble."

The consul suggested she go to Nanjiang to settle her plans with the Chinese government, but since her husband's scientific credentials had been questioned and Smith's badgering had been ignored, she rightly figured that a totally inexperienced woman would get even less consideration. She found more satisfaction making friends with a ricksha driver who gave tours around Beijing. He even brought her to his home for tea and to meet his family.

Then she relented and traveled to Nanjiang anyway, but before she had a chance to talk to any relevant or irrelevant bureaucrats, she took ill with bronchitis and returned to

Shanghai to recover. Perhaps she'd spent too much time around Smith already and had caught a dose of his hypochondria, because her bronchitis turned into dysentery, and she spent the better part of August in a hospital.

She was still at a loss of how to capture pandas, so she amused herself with small delights: She discovered a tailor who could take the silks she bought for pennies and the designs she drew and turn them into dresses that cost her a mere couple of dollars. Essentially she was languishing in Shanghai, even farther from panda country than her husband had got.

She was rescued by Arthur Sowerby, the editor of *China Journal*, who threw a party at his house on her behalf and introduced her to Jack Young. Young's wife Su Lin worked at the journal, and Jack had met Bill Harkness in New York when he had just returned from the East Indies. (In his old age, all that Jack Young could remember of that meeting was that Bill Harkness wore a beard, as one would expect of a returning explorer.) A day later, Young called Harkness at the Palace Hotel and arranged to meet with her. Harkness's description of him fit him to a tee:

"He was a slim, wiry young man whose black eyes sparkled, and whose whole frame seemed to vibrate when he talked of the snow-capped mountains that lie range on range west of Chengtu, rising to meet the high Tibetan plateaus. He talked of the little-known valleys to the south of Tatsienlu, and as he talked it became a living land of romance to me."

Harkness knew that Young's wife Su Lin had accompanied him on a recent trip and therefore she asked how Mrs. Young had withstood the rigors of the trail. Jack Young, of course, said she had done very well.

That evening, Jack Young had a talk with his brother, Quentin. Jack was already heading out on expedition with Arthur Emmons, one of the mountaineers from the Minya Konka climb. They were going to attempt a first ascent of Nanda Devi in the Himalayas. Quentin was nervous about meeting the American woman. Jack told him not to worry; she'd listen to him, and besides, they'd be going to their old hunting grounds near Tatsienlu where Quentin already knew everyone.

"Why don't you take a year off and take care of this," Jack told him, "Make some money, and to hell with whether you're successful or not."

Quentin had some other ideas.

"All he wanted was to get a giant panda for himself," Jack Young recalled. "He wants to get a giant panda for the museum. He has no interest in money."

The brotherly competition kicked in. Ruth Harkness wrote that Jack Young had shot a panda by the time she reached China; Jack Young told me that he had not. He'd bought panda pelts and skeletons for the American Museum of Natural History in New York and for the Royal Asiatic Society Museum in Shanghai.

Quentin was going to do him one better and shoot one himself for the Academia Sinica in Nanjiang. He talked it over with his girlfriend Diana. She reminded him that he only had a semester left in school. She told him that he didn't need to take up the expedition just for money because she had enough for both of them, given that her parents in the Dutch East Indies sent her plenty. But if he wanted to go to make a name for himself, then he should do it. She knew well that Quentin was as jealous of her fame as an athlete as he was of his brother's reputation as an explorer.

Besides, he was idealistic—and even more, nationalistic. He wanted a Chinese to capture a panda for China, not a foreigner. He'd grown up among foreigners, been educated by foreigners, read about the exploits of foreigners. And above all, he knew that those foreigners regarded him as just another "Chink." He was going to do something to make them take notice.

The next day, Jack had a letter delivered to Harkness at the hotel to let her know that his little brother Quentin might be willing to guide her to panda country. He arranged a meeting. Quentin was a bundle of nerves, and Jack tried to pour confidence into him, reminding him that there would be no one else on the trip but him and this foreign woman. Of course, that's exactly why Quentin was nervous. He didn't like foreigners, for one thing. And the last trip had been so perilous because of bandits and warring factions. Now he'd be responsible for a foreign woman's safety through that chaos.

"Don't belittle yourself," Jack barked. "You must show her that you are competent."

Ruth was waiting for him in the bar at the Palace Hotel. They were both shocked at first sight, he by her New York detachment, she because he was younger, more handsome, and with his western haircut and suit, much less foreign than she had expected of a Chinese hunter. His description of her was all yin and yang.

"She had lipstick all over her," he told me, "and I don't like the turban she wore. But her character is impressive. She is 13 years older than me, but she doesn't look so old. She is very pleasant, but she smokes a lot."

Harkness's recollection of Quentin from that first meeting was far kinder.

"As I walked down the lobby, the tallest Chinese lad I have ever seen rose from a chair in the far end of the lounge and came toward me," she wrote. "He was just under six feet tall, and there was something vaguely familiar about the rather slouchy, long-legged stride. It puzzled me all the time I was talking to him, which was most of the afternoon, until suddenly I realized what it was. He made me think of Brother Jim—the same droop of the shoulder, the long loose stride, and the same kind of shy smile that Jim had when he was twenty. Quentin was not much over that."

She told him that she didn't have much money to pay him with—she actually had $1,000 in US currency that she kept in a little cash box, a nice tidy sum. He assured her that the cost of living in the interior was quite cheap. They settled on $200 a month, and the low wages suited Quentin because he felt less restricted. He could do his own hunting as well.

The next day, Harkness met with both of the Young brothers. They brought maps to show her the lay of the land south of Tatsienlu on the flanks of Minya Konka. She wasn't so much interested in the maps and the details as in the stories of lamas and high passes and bamboo forests. Jack did most of the talking, mapping out a voyage down to where the Roosevelts had shot their panda. Quentin mostly listened.

Harkness bragged in her book—and elsewhere—that she'd skirted the Chinese regulations. In fact Jack and Quentin Young had cut a deal with the Academia Sinica. The travel permits for obtaining one live giant panda would cost one dead panda for the museum.

The bulk of Bill Harkness's supplies were warehoused in a garage in Shanghai's French concession, and Quentin set to methodically inventorying them. He threw out the maggot-infested foodstuffs, counted out the parkas and boots and socks and set aside what they needed. There were quite a few firearms. Quentin picked out a .38 caliber revolver he thought Harkness should carry, but she shrank from it. The medical supplies also gave her a fright: the drugs, the syringes, the scalpels, the canisters of ether for anesthesia—just in case they had to amputate something. She wondered what she was getting into.

Quentin had traps built, giant contraptions of wood and chain that would tighten around a leg and firmly yet gently hold a big animal. Catching the panda, he and Jack agreed, would be easier than transporting it out of the forest.

Harkness, for her part, set out the smallest of her husband's clothing—suit coats, slacks, even woolen underwear—and took them to her tailor, who cut them down so expertly that they delighted the sophisticated New York dress designer. She found a shoemaker who miraculously did the same with a pair of Bill's hobnailed boots.

One evening, Jack and Su Lin Young came to dine at the Palace Hotel. Jack Young, the great arranger, was taking good care of her. Harkness was more fascinated by Mrs. Young, whom she described glowingly, as a magazine's style editor might describe a model in a fashion show:

"Tiny, with just a suggestion of chubbiness; sleek beautifully waved hair, and sparkling black eyes. She wore the modern Chinese woman's costume which, as Bill had written, is at the same time the most demure and the most seductive garb imaginable. A straight slim Chinese coat with high collar, falling to the ankles, but slit to the knees to show twinkling little feet and slender silk-stockinged legs, and a glimpse of the lovely handmade petticoats that are cut exactly like that outer skirt. Su Lin, like many modern Chinese girls, makes the average American girl's make-up look crude and blatant. Her pale ivory skin was faintly shaded with a peach blossom tint, so exquisitely that I did not know until much later that it was rouge. I looked at this delicate bit of femininity who barely came to my shoulder, and decided that certainly if she could stand the rigors of a Tibetan expedition, so could I."

Jack Young remembered that part of the conversation.

"Can you stand lice?" he asked her.

Harkness pointed to Su Lin and said, "If she can stand it, I can too."

She was enchanted by all things Chinese, especially the Young family.

She wrote:"It was fun being with Quentin, Jack and Su Lin, the latter two always vivacious and sparkling; Quentin in contrast with his brother's nervous, quick speech and movements, his bubbling enthusiasms, was shy and quiet, saying little."

And both brothers stood in great contrast to Floyd Smith. Just days before she and Quentin headed upriver, Smith came to Harkness's hotel room and sat on a steamer trunk drinking "his pre-luncheon whiskey-soda," while still trying to talk some sense into Harkness. Smith wanted to come along, but she wouldn't have it. He still thought she was foolish to only hunt pandas when there were so many other marketable creatures out there on the Sichuan-Tibetan border.

Perhaps that is when they talked about the alleged agreement he referred to later, an agreement that she'd stay out of his hunting territories. At the time it was not an issue, because his camp was in the Zhaopo Valley and the Youngs intended to take Harkness farther south, beyond Tatsienlu.

Quentin Young never met Smith and felt that Smith avoided him whenever he came to the Palace Hotel. He also thought Harkness resented Smith because she suspected he'd been a partner in her husband's demise.

"She told me she hates that Zoology Jones," Quentin Young said during our interviews. He tended to use Harkness's depreciative nickname whenever he spoke of Smith, but I never thought to ask if that's how he and Harkness referred to him on the trail or if Harkness thought up the name later and he only read it in her book. But he went on and on about Smith and why Harkness hated him.

"Why? Because to my observation she strongly thought that Zoology Jones was trying to dope Bill with drinks, women, and all that so that Zoology can control the whole thing and boss the whole expedition financially and publicity and all that."

Jack Young thought Harkness realized that Smith was in great financial need and was trying to sell Harkness's equipment to maintain his foreigner's lifestyle. Harkness never said so in her book, making only a veiled reference to the accounts between Smith and Bill Harkness that were never really straightened out.

But in that scene in her hotel room, Harkness showed she was far ahead of her time in her intolerance of racism. She held "Zoology Jones" in disdain as an example of why she didn't want any other foreigners on her expedition.

" . . . I had seen enough of the attitude of most Westerners in China to heartily resent it," she wrote.

"Why, because of the difference in the color of a skin people sweepingly think of themselves as superior beings, I could not understand, and still don't. The infinite patience the Chinese have with our assumption of authority and superiority in their own country is one of the amazing things of this world. We are guests in a strange land; we do nothing but criticize an ancient cultured race, beside whom we are crude children—barbarians—and expect our hosts not to resent us. I began to divide Westerners into just two classes, and like or dislike them accordingly—those in whom the Chinese found something to like, and those in whom they could not. And China is generous—to those who give, she returns in brimming measure."

Her own cup was about to overflow.

A floating bridge. Courtesy Mrs. Vivan Dai.

CHAPTER EIGHT

UPRIVER

Harriet Anderson described her older sister Ruth Harkness as a romantic who saw things as she chose to see them. That, anyway, was her explanation for Harkness's penchant for leaving out some details and changing others. She'd left out the circumstances of her husband's death, for example, which only made readers suspect worse things than really happened. While in China, she was greatly aided by the generosity of Standard Oil executives, but for baffling reasons, in her book she referred to the company as "Gascony" and not "Socony" (Standard Oil Company of New York), even though she later made a fuss when people she met assumed that she was a member of the Harkness family that co-owned Socony. She was not; Bill's family was prominent, but was not involved in Standard Oil. Ruth had apparently schmoozed her way into the good graces of the company's managers in China, which was not necessarily difficult to do, given the camaraderie among foreigners in China.

One of the more unexplainable fabrications Harkness made in her book is the statement that there was another panda expedition that left for the interior three weeks before she did. It couldn't have been Smith; if he wasn't already in the hospital, he soon would be, because his correspondence to Chicago places him there at the end of October.

Anderson told me that her sister, Ruth Harkness, kept journals and that they'd been passed on to her, and she gave me two different explanations of what had happened to them. One was that as she reached old age and went into a retirement home, she'd given power of attorney to a trusted friend who she thought had burned many of her private things, including Ruth's papers. The other explanation was that she'd passed them on to her and Harkness's niece Jane Jones, who was only about four years younger than Anderson. Jones said she'd never seen any journals, which is too bad, because the fictions and embellishments that Harkness wrote into her book seriously damaged her credibility and Quentin Young's credibility as well. And if she didn't seem to care, those questions have plagued Young for the rest of his life. But of course, one didn't divulge certain things in the 1930s because the scandal threshold was so much lower. People behaved as they have always behaved, but for better or worse, they didn't feel they had to talk about it.

Harkness spent her last weeks in Shanghai at night clubs and farewell parties, and although she was impressed by what a cosmopolitan city it was, it just didn't fit into the image of China that she wanted to experience. She wanted to flee from everything she knew, and she would soon be on her way to doing just that.

Quentin Young had decided that they should travel by boat instead of flying to Chengdu. They had far too much equipment and luggage for the aircraft of that time and place. But more importantly, arriving by plane would be far too conspicuous. If he and Harkness called too much attention to themselves, they'd get passed around among all the local government officials along the way and subjected to made-up visas and taxes and permits. That was essentially what had happened to Bill Harkness, even with Floyd Smith's expertise as an "Old China Hand."

Instead they booked passage on a steamer up the Yangsi and set sail late on the night of September 26, 1936. They each had their own send-off parties. Harkness's was attended by her new-found Shanghai friends, each of them spouting jokes about the unlikelihood of her venture.

Harkness, however, kept her eyes on Young's party, which she described as: "a good-looking bunch of athletic youngsters." Just as she had been impressed by Su Lin Young, she was again taken by how modern these Chinese women seemed. "There was one girl in particular, who caught my attention—a tall striking-looking person with sleek bobbed hair, wearing a brilliant red sweater; the type of modern Chinese girl, completely unknown in Shanghai a generation ago," she continued. "These girls had their freedom just as the boys did, and seemed to react to it in exactly the same way as a group of American youngsters would."

The "girl in the red sweater," of course, was Diana Chen, Young's girlfriend, and Harkness always referred to her that way, even while on the trail. Her jealousy was welling up, not just over Young, but over the China she wanted to embrace, the primitive, foreign world she'd find upriver.

It took them three days to reach Hankow, camped out on the deck of the steamer while the Chinese travelers stacked and packed into the lower levels of the ship. Harkness was struck by their seeming resignation to the squalor and the cramped quarters. She saw it as a sign of nobility and wisdom.

She loved the bustling confusion of the river towns they stopped in, where the ship could take on freight and passengers. She loved the commotion, the cacophony of Chinese dialects, and the crowds she inevitably gathered wherever she went. She was as much an oddity to the people she met as they were to her. She remarked to Young that she wouldn't know what to do if she ever got separated from him in one of those towns, and he quipped, "I'd just look for you where the biggest crowd had collected, and I'd know you'd be there." She asked Young to teach her Chinese, but she couldn't quite get her mind or her mouth around the complex tones and inflections.

"She was quite busy with her typewriter," Young remembered. "I thought it was quite silly."

She would pepper him with questions: how much they spent for lunch; what they had eaten; and other things. Of course she was already writing a book, or maybe just keeping a diary, since she'd never before in her life had any sort of literary or journalistic inclination.

"By the time I first read the book, I was amazed," Young said many years later. "How can that woman describe all those things. How could she take so much interest in those things? I should have told her more."

At the time, he thought she asked far too much. She'd brought a stocked bar with her luggage, and every night after she cleaned up—on the trail, as on board ship—she'd mix cocktails. She taught Young how to drink Manhattans at first, and then martinis.

"Quentin, come here and talk to me," she'd say.

"Why?"

"I don't want to think about anything," she'd reply. Or, "I'm lonesome. Nobody understands me."

Then she'd start long cat-and-mouse conversations, prying information out of the shy young man, questions about his girlfriend, about his peculiar name, and other things. When he'd come up with questions of his own—how old she was, for example—she'd drop her voice into its lowest registers and with a mock pout, say, "You're not supposed to ask. I'm your big sister." In fact, she was his boss, and he kept his patience with her.

The Yangsi was wide and muddy between Shanghai and Hankow, and it was filled with every shape and size of watercraft. But from Hankow inland it narrowed and became more difficult to navigate and they had to change ships.

Harkness had made arrangements to travel farther upstream on a Socony tanker delivering kerosene for lighting to the big cities upriver. But the tanker was delayed, and so they spent three nights in Hankow. Young made himself scarce, happy to be away from her questions. She attended parties in her honor while dressed in her finest expedition clothing, which, from her description sounds rather like a precursor to Chairman Mao's wardrobe. While among the foreigners of Hankow, she fended off so many allusions to Standard Oil—on whose ship she would be traveling—that she threatened to put a sign on her back saying that she wasn't one of *those* Harknesses, again referring to the last name she shared with the oil barons.

Back on the water, Harkness found marvel in everything she saw: the ship's captain's experience and dedication, even the dull landscape along the shore. They reached the city of Ichang by October 8, and the river became even more interesting to her. The ship had to gun its engines to fight upstream through the rapids. As they steamed and struggled up gorges cut hundreds of feet through rock by seasonal surges of the river, she noticed the naked men walking along towpaths high up the cliff walls, pulling junks upstream with long ropes.

Four days later they reached Chonqing, where they spent the night in a Socony warehouse. The Standard Oil executives had also arranged for Harkness and Young to travel the last 300 miles in a private car while their luggage followed behind on a bus. Harkness was astounded to find a road at all, however bumpy. But at least it passed through the kind of pre-twentieth century landscape she yearned for, past rice paddies and rolling agricultural lands.

It took two days on the road to reach the walled city of Chengdu, where they'd pick up the last of Bill Harkness's provisions before heading south toward Tatsienlu. They stayed at the rambling old home of E. A. Cavaliere, an Italian who served as the customs commissioner for Sichuan. Since the Boxer Rebellion, China had conceded its customs authority and other potentially profitable services to European nations, which only added to Chinese citizens' resentment of foreigners. Curiously, though she includes Cavaliere's name among the dedications in the front of her book, over the body of the text she changes his name to "Caballero."

Cavaliere was one of the few Westerners—other than missionaries—who lived in Chengdu, and because he received and forwarded mail for foreigners in the region, American and European travelers visiting Chengdu naturally gravitated to his home. This suited Young, because there were plenty of Europeans to occupy Harkness, and he could easily disappear into the city to spend time alone and clear his head.

But from her descriptions, Harkness's Chengdu society conversations mostly consisted of warnings from all of the

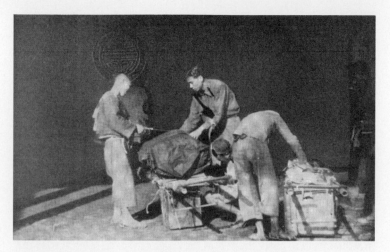

Quentin Young (center) sorts equipment in the courtyard of the customs commissioner's house in Chengdu. From Ruth Harkness's collection, courtesy Mary Lobisco.

Westerners regarding how foolish she was to think of trekking into the forest with a single companion. They told her she might not return at all, which didn't seem to upset her nearly as much as when Cavaliere suddenly bolted from the house with a shotgun to shoot a stray cat off his roof. The cat's claws were putting holes in the roof tiles and making the roof leak, he explained. One wonders what the buckshot did to the tiles, but at any rate, Harkness was shocked at the barbarity.

To Young's great dismay, Cavaliere convinced Harkness to change her destination. He knew of pandas sighted up near the village of Zhaopo. That, after all, is where Dean Sage shot his, and where Harkness's husband had been headed with Floyd Smith. Young had expected to go his old hunting grounds where he knew his way around and where he knew the local hunters and the local authorities. Now he was heading into unfamiliar territory. Harkness had made up her mind and she was the boss.

On Cavaliere's recommendation, they hired a Chengdu cook named Wang, a man as jolly as a fat man is supposed to be. And they hired coolies to carry their gear. There was a primitive motor road from Chengdu that went at least as far as Wenchuan, but it was closed to cars other than those belonging to the local warlord or to dignitaries who had his express permission to use it. And though there was a bus that ran once a day, it was usually far too full to accommodate Young, Harkness, *and* their 22 pieces of luggage. So Young haggled with local residents until he had hired 16 men to carry them and their gear for 110 miles across the Chengdu plain and up into the mountains. The coolies hung the luggage from poles that spanned from one man's shoulders to another's on a contraption they called a Wha-gar.

The caravan set out from Chengdu on October 19. Harkness rode in a Wha-gar rigged with a seat. Occasionally she walked to try to get herself in shape, but she couldn't keep up with the coolies, even though they were half her size and carried twice her weight. Her feet blistered in her husband's cut-down hobnailed boots, and she eventually gave them up and wore rope sandals like the coolies wore. She never complained and instead seemed to revel in the discomfort, waxing eloquent about the endless parade of humanity on that dusty road through the fields.

"I like her courage, her stubbornness," Young told me.

They stopped at teahouses for meals, and at night they stayed in roadside inns, which were often little more than damp rabbit-warren cubicles. The inns were infested with bedbugs, so she and Young would let the coolies scramble into the cubicles and then set her cot in the courtyard or other public areas.

The first night they stopped at an inn, Harkness noticed the sweet smell drifting in from another room and asked Young what it was.

"You don't know?" he answered.

The innkeeper was an opium smoker, and Harkness wanted to try it. Young was aghast. He was an ardent follower of Chiang Kaishek and his New Life campaign, one of whose tenets was to discourage opium smoking. Harkness ignored his protests and smoked—and she liked its calming sense of well being.

But Young would never let her smoke it again. Nearly from the start of the trek, Young fought with the coolies over their opium habits. Midway through the day, some of them would start to turn pale and stagger and have to stop to find a fix before they could continue. He tried limiting their wages to just enough money to eat, but they'd forego food and buy opium instead. In the mornings, Young would have to rouse them all, sometimes at gun point to get them moving. Several ran away, which meant that there were no longer enough porters to man the Wha-gars. They had to resort to wheelbarrows—and at times, Young even rode in a wheelbarrow himself.

Finally, realizing it was a losing battle, Young gave up and let the coolies smoke, stopping deliberately before steep pitches so that the opium smokers among them could light up and fortify themselves for the climb. When the terrain became more rugged, Harkness would take care that the coolies carrying her Wha-gar were not opium smokers, because the trail was so narrow and precipitous in places that her seat swung out over the cliffs.

On the second morning out of Chengdu, they saw contingents of soldiers racing here and there. They were chasing bandits, and they had caught two ringleaders. A company of soldiers

The gate to Guanxian. From Ruth Harkness's collection, courtesy Mary Lobisco.

rushed them past Young and Harkness's caravan, hogtied, one of the bandits walking, the other seated in a wheelbarrow. A short time later, by the side of the road, they came upon the body of one of those bandits, his face full of bullet holes. His comrades had ambushed the soldiers in an attempt to rescue him, and the soldiers had shot their prisoner dead rather than let him escape. The other bandit apparently had escaped. Harkness looked on impassively, wondering why this scene bothered her less than when Cavaliere had shot the cat off his roof.

"We expected things to happen at any minute," Young said. "She doesn't understand how dangerous it was. Not until she had seen those bandits killed did she realize that it was no fun. It was real and she listened to me."

In the town of Guanxian, she ran into a League of Nations representative whom she'd met at Cavaliere's house. He was out in the countryside on official business—traveling by car, of course, as befitted his diplomatic standing. She filled him with stories of her adventures, which apparently he brought back to Chengdu.

From Guanxian, the trail started to climb. Early the next day they ran into another company of soldiers on the road who would not let them pass. Harkness assumed that her trip was done, that she was being ordered back to safer environs, and she sat, dejected as she listened to Young argue with them in Chinese. In fact, a general in Chengdu had sent orders to his troops in Guanxian that they were to accompany the caravan as escorts and protect them against bandits. Still not wanting to create a noticeable commotion, Young talked half of them into turning back.

Harkness, of course, loved the commotion, and she gladly worked the soldiers into her traveling celebration, listening to Young's translations of their made-up stories about pandas, smoking cigarettes with them and making them laugh by taking target practice with their weapons.

They reached Wenchuan a day or so later and camped in a crumbling, abandoned Buddhist temple. In the morning, Young asked her if she had slept well, which of course, she had. Then he told her that someone had tried to rob them during the night, but he'd driven them off. And with that he finally convinced her to carry a .38 revolver in case of emergency.

Wenchuan was the last major town they'd pass through on the way to panda country, and so Young started to look for hunters. He was approached by one of the hunters Smith kept there on retainer. Harkness didn't even change the hunter's name when she described him in her book.

"A certain Wang of the town came to him and offered his services," she wrote. "Wang, it seemed, was Zoology's hunter, who lived very nicely in the town without bothering himself much about going out to hunt. He informed Quentin that he knew that he was still being paid each month from money that had been sent to Zoology by the foreign devil's husband before he died, but that made no difference—for still more he would work for us. 'That,' said Quentin in disgust, 'is what some foreigners call 'the Chinese mind.' So we decided that as long as we had secured porters we would continue the next morning and trust to luck to find honest and efficient hunters up in the mountains."

Sixty years later, Young was of the same mind when he angrily said to me, "Smith's people? Whose people? These are Chinese people. How can you say his people? They work for anyone who comes along."

Further, he says they were likely fooling Smith by telling him that hunting was far more difficult work than he could imagine—especially if he was paying them day to day. Finding a panda under those circumstances would take many, many days.

Young had decided instead to hire hunters when he reached the mountains, but one found him first, an old Tibetan headman with an older blunderbuss rifle. His name was Lao Tsang, and here is Harkness's description:

"Wild gray hair escaping from a dirty white turban carelessly slipping over one ear," she wrote, "an ancient skin coat with the fur inside, something made of leather that was half boots and half gaiters was held up to his waist by strings and over it all a loose homespun garment bunched up around him with a rope. He tethered two mongrel dogs with tinkling bells to the foot of the ladder and mumbling to himself mounted to the loft.

Harkness and her military escort check into the temple at Wenchuan. From Ruth Harkness's collection, courtesy Mary Lobisco.

"'How old do you suppose he is,' I asked in astonishment, as I caught a glimpse of his leathery face and his toothless mouth.

"'Oh, at least Ming dynasty,' returned Quentin."

The trail from Wenchuan was rugged and poorly marked, through deep forest, bamboo thickets and occasional pine stands. "Lots of up and down, I tell you. It is difficult," Young said. It took two days to reach the next village. Along the way, they found panda droppings, a good omen.

"We had climbed, scrambled and fallen over nearly thirty miles of country that day," Harkness wrote of finally reaching Zhaopo. It was a village of 45 or 50 people—except when the warlord's troops came to draft more soldiers. Then it had fewer people, because they ran away to hide or to join the Communists. They grew potatoes and dug for herbs to make a living. Finding panda hunters among them was not so easy.

"That place was new to me," Young told me. "They hunt for a living, not for panda but for other animals. They sell them for pelts and clothing. They don't hunt panda because the meat doesn't taste good, and the fur is not good. It's too coarse."

About the only reason they might have had to shoot a panda—if they even knew what a panda was—was if it raided their village. Young and Harkness listened to all sorts of imaginative and nonsensical accounts of pandas told to them by villagers, including tales of pandas wandering into the local school. Young had no tolerance for tomfoolery, however, and he would bully and cajole the hunters just as he had done with the coolies, threatening to run them before the magistrate if they tried any tricks.

There was a deserted castle in Zhaopo, a remnant of a kingdom that had been called Wassu, and they set up camp there. It was a three-story building with pagoda-like eves and a tall watch tower built into the side of a hill. Inside, Harkness described finding: "all manner of fascinating things left by the Lamas who had occupied the place before the same defeated army that ruined Wenchuan had passed through. [. . .]

"In the upper reaches were galaxies of gods, their bright colors dimmed by the dust of neglect. Someone later referred to them as obscene, which rather astonished me, as they so obviously and frankly represented a worship of life and reproduction that one took it as they were meant."

Young was one of the people who found them obscene. There was a secret compartment in the castle, filled with statues of deities engaged in all sorts of sex acts.

"Let's get away from this place before they catch us and tell us we can't stay here anymore," Young claimed he told her.

But the suggestive statues gave Harkness ideas of her own, "put her in the mood," as Young described it. And he gave in to her, as any man might have. But the guilt of it drove him off into the forests to scout their new hunting grounds. He was gone three days. Harkness stayed at the camp in the castle, fiddling with her typewriter and smoking the last of her cigarettes. They would only spend a week in panda country.

Quentin Young beneath the castle at Zhaopo. Courtesy June Young.

CHAPTER NINE

THE CATCH

"Mr. Young, Madame is drunk again."

It was the fat cook, Wang, come to tell Young that Harkness wanted him. There was a knowing smile on his face. *Yang tai-tai* was the word Wang used to describe Harkness. *Tai-tai* means "Mrs."; *Yang* means, "foreigner," "over the ocean." With another inflection it was Young's Chinese name, and Wang played with the pun, deliberately making it sound as if Young and Harkness were husband and wife. It's hard to keep secrets on the trail, after all. On the cold nights they'd had to share blankets—and more. While he was pursuing pandas, she was pursuing the panda hunter.

Even as an old man, he was blushingly romantic. Back then, he'd been a conservative young man engaged to a proper Chinese girl from a prominent family. He obviously regretted the affair with Harkness, however fleeting. He brought it up in our first interview, but always spoke in couched terms, and later regretted he'd mentioned it altogether. Certainly it would have been scandalous in 1936: an American widow having sex out of wedlock with a much younger Chinese man. Young claimed that he didn't even find her attractive.

"The first thing I don't like is her looks," he said, but then later acceded, "I like her courage, her stubbornness, but she's not my same race. It's hard to look at a person from a different culture. For me it was not the standard of Oriental women of those days. Now they are about the same."

Young left Harkness at the Zhaopo castle to go scout their hunting grounds. She passed the time with her typewriter and with the cook and the hunters, whom she described as if they were silly children. They liked to play with her flashlight, to get into her things, to distract her in so many ways. Young set up two camps in the mountains above Zhaopo, one for her and another for himself. He'd placed hers on the only flat spot he could find within a day's climb from Zhaopo at 8,000 feet in elevation. He'd made a cook shack out of the remains of an old dwelling, and set up the tropical tent that Bill Harkness had used in the Philippines. It wasn't warm enough for the coming winter weather, but it was big enough to put her cot in, a welcome bit of privacy after the too-close and too-open chaos of the castle in Zhaopo. By the time they'd moved her gear into the campsite, however, it was snowing hard. The porters and the hunters couldn't make it to their own homes or camps, so 23 of them spent the night huddled together for warmth near the fire in the cook shack.

In the morning, Young staged a flag-raising ceremony at the lower camp. He'd bought American and Chinese flags in Shanghai, the American flag for her camp and the Chinese flag for his own camp at 11,000 feet. After the ceremony he took off for the higher camp, ostensibly to scout the area.

Over the next few days, he and the hunters built bridges across the streams for Harkness's eventual arrival at the high camp. They set up traps. Young read letters from Diana that had been delivered on a roundabout route from Chengdu. She'd set several track and field records for China in international events while he'd been gone.

Homesick, perhaps feeling a bit guilty about his infidelities, he used a finger to write her name in the snow on his tent. Then he set his camera on a tripod and snapped his picture standing next to the lettered tent and staring off into the distance, stalwart as a superhero.

Harkness stayed at the lower camp, puttering around at what she called "housewifely" duties, working at her typewriter and watching the trail for Young's red hunting cap. Wang the cook made scones for her—something he'd learned while working in a French restaurant in Chengdu. However, he'd never learned how to pronounce the word, and instead called them "skonks."

It was bitter cold, so Harkness sat in the cook shack to stay warm, but that left her exposed to the insatiable curiosity of one of the hunters' wives, who followed her around. Harkness became increasingly annoyed with the woman's hawking and spitting. And after a few days she became bored and insisted on going hunting with Young.

Harkness called the Sichuan landscape, "a lovely lost world of tumbled mountains." She couldn't believe that rhododendrons could grow so tall, or that bamboo could grow so thick. November already: the aspen was burning gold amid the red and orange leaves of other deciduous trees. It had been snowing in Young's camp, and Harkness noticed with each morning that the snow line crept farther and farther down the mountainsides.

The trails—what passed for trails, anyway—were treacherously rocked and gullied, and they were slick from the rain and snow. She struggled to get up them. Young deliberately took the most difficult routes he could find with the hope that Harkness would give up and stay in camp. He'd push her and pull her— "I don't know: I think she likes it." —then he'd natter, telling her she was a nuisance when she couldn't keep up. But she earned his grudging admiration anyway because she wouldn't quit.

"She sticks to it like a leech," he said.

Once, in a particularly nasty thicket, the bamboo spines tore Ruth's pants from her backside and Quentin had to wrap his shirt around her. Even sixty years later, as he told the story, he turned his head to one side and winced as if he were averting his eyes. He had to take her back to camp to change clothes. Though she found it terribly amusing, Young did not—at least not with the passage of years.

Regardless of how much Young would complain about Harkness's attentions and ineptitudes, I found it hard to believe him. She was too likable. In her book, she never once suggests that Young was rude or in any way unpleasant to her. But then again, she wasn't going to let anything ruin her quest.

They'd only been at the high camp a few days when they found their panda. November 9 was snowy and cold, and they had to climb up a thousand feet through low-hanging clouds and through underbrush so soaked that it was "a shower bath at every touch." Harkness tried to light a cigarette, but she didn't have a dry match, and even if she had had one, the very air was too wet to allow the fire any chance at igniting the cigarette tobacco.

They had hoped to trap a giant panda. The pelts that native hunters brought to white explorers had mostly been caught in traps that triggered spring-loaded spears and killed the animal that stepped into it. Young had brought humane traps that he'd rigged from bear traps. They were making the rounds of those set traps, looking to see if they'd caught anything, when the shots rang out.

"Without warning a shout went up from the jungle ahead of us," Harkness wrote. "I heard Lao Tsang yell, the report of his blunderbuss musket, and then Quentin's voice raised in rapid and imperious Chinese. Falling, stumbling or being dragged by Yang we crashed through the bamboo. I caught a glimpse of Quentin through the almost impenetrable wet green wall, and got close enough to gasp, 'What is it?'

"*Bei-shung*," was the terse reply."

Young was furious. Lao Tsang later told him that in the heat of the hunt, he'd forgotten the orders not to shoot. Young didn't believe him, but apparently didn't say anything to Harkness.

George Schaller, the wildlife biologist who helped set up the Chinese government's panda study at the Wolong preserve, told me that the local hunters would certainly have known enough about pandas to simply check every hollow tree during the panda birthing season. Young and Harkness would not have known that, nor would they necessarily have known if the hunters were deliberately leading them in that direction.

Young felt that Lao Tsang and his men had shot the mother panda, hid it, skinned it, and probably ate it. When he heard the shots, he charged uphill, but then had to stop to wait for Harkness, lest he lose her in the forest.

"Hey, where are you?" he called down to her.

"I'm coming."

Then he heard something. Here's Harkness's description:

"Quentin stopped so short that I almost fell over him. He listened intently for a split second and then went plowing on so rapidly I couldn't keep up to him. Dimly through the waving wet branches I saw him near a huge rotting tree. I stumbled on blindly brushing the water from my face and eyes. Then I too stopped, frozen in my tracks. From the old dead tree came a baby's whimper.

"I must have been momentarily paralyzed, for I didn't move until Quentin came toward me and held out his arms. There in the palms of his two hands was a squirming baby *bei-shung*."

It was the size of a puppy and weighed two to three pounds. Young and Harkness thought it was just a few days old because its eyes were not yet open. But it was probably about a month old, because, as George Schaller has since told me, giant panda babies don't open their eyes until a month and a half after birth.

Young wanted to put it back in the tree, but Harkness took it to her breast and cuddled it like a human baby.

"Oh, I'm going to find those fools," Young ranted. "I'm not going to pay them because I told them not to shoot any panda."

Harkness cut him off.

"No, no, no," she said. "This is what I want."

Young was even more distressed. He'd brought those giant traps and cages. He wanted a full-grown panda. The baby would die before they got it back to civilization, he told her. But she'd already anticipated this. She had brought a baby bottle on the trip. It was packed into one of their trunks back in camp.

Her account of the find never mentions the debate with Young. Instead, she fast forwards to Young putting the baby animal inside his shirt and the two of them sliding and staggering back down to Young's camp.

Young dug the baby bottle out of the trunk and had the cook heat water for powdered milk. When the panda didn't seem to be able to suck, they widened the hole in the nipple. The panda took the bottle.

Shortly after they returned to camp, they heard the hunters shouting. Young had to run into the forest to rescue Lao Tsang, who had been treed by a wild boar. For the rest of the evening, the wild boar story proved more interesting to the native hunters than the baby panda.

Young and Harkness worried over the tiny animal. Nobody had ever cared for one before, after all. They fed it every six or seven hours. Harkness later told *China Journal* that Young even turned his shearling coat inside out to pretend to be a mother panda and thus better encourage the baby to nurse from the bottle. Harkness decided to name it Su Lin after Jack Young's wife, not just in homage, but because it truly was a "a little bit something cute."

The next day, they brought the animal down to the lower camp. Harkness wanted to go native: She led the hunters into the woods so that they could sacrifice a rooster to the mountain gods. They slit the bird's throat, set off firecrackers, and burned money, and one wonders how much of that was for the hunters and how much was for Harkness's benefit.

More questions: Harkness wanted to know why they set out three glasses of wine for the mountain gods. Young had to ask the hunters, who explained that the glasses represented offerings to heaven, earth, and humanity. He suddenly realized that he was learning things from her inquisitive ways.

Young told me that once they had captured their baby panda, Harkness suggested that they make a baby of their own.

Su Lin, the panda, begins her journey to Chengdu in a basket on a porter's back. From Ruth Harkness's collection, courtesy Mary Lobisco.

Young didn't admit whether he agreed. But in keeping with the morality of the era, she later told Arthur Sowerby something quite different.

"We have it on the authority of Mrs. Harkness that, so great were their emotions, the only thing they could do was solemnly to shake hands," he wrote.

There was more ceremony to come. Early the next morning, Harkness and Young climbed back uphill so that Harkness could bury her husband's cremated remains in a little cardboard box beneath a rhododendron tree. The next day they limped back to Zhaopo—Harkness slipped on the trail and sprained a hip. And the day after that they sprinted back to Wenchuan.

Floyd Smith's man, Wang, apparently had already heard the news of the panda and he came to meet them, insisting on throwing a feast for them that very night. Harkness hinted in her book that Wang might have incited soldiers to try to keep them from leaving town. Young told me he was more than a little worried about being kidnapped, and so they left town before the feast was over.

They hired porters for the caravan back to Chengdu, but the porters proved so incompetent—or perhaps Young and Harkness were so impatient to get back—that Young fired them. Somehow he'd procured a pony in Wenchuan, and so he and Harkness took turns riding it while the four hunters with them took turns carrying the panda in a backpack.

Once again they piled into roadside inns, and Harkness bemoaned the lack of privacy. In an amusing aside, she describes cutting off a pair of overripe underpants with a knife because she had nowhere to change them. She threw them away in a corner, but then found the hunters had picked them up and folded them back into her luggage. After several days of playing lost and found with the hunters and the discarded underpants, she threw them off a cliff to keep them from returning again.

The little caravan stopped at an inn just short of Guanxian, hoping to avoid the big-city crowds they had attracted even before they had a baby panda. They sent a runner ahead to the Chengdu to bring word to Cavaliere, the customs commissioner there, and ask him to meet them in Guanxian to drive them to Chengdu in his car. This would save them two days of walking.

That night, Harkness made a last attempt at expressing her gratitude to Young.

"My recollection of the last inn is now vague, except for the conversation that kept us up later than usual," she wrote. "Food and to bed at six or seven was the rule, but this evening I tried in a stumbling way to tell Quentin what a joy the whole trip had been, what the new world that had been opened to me meant—what complete happiness I had found, and that I was more than grateful to him for his share in it. It was difficult, so I merely gave him a carved gold ring for the Girl in the Red Sweater and wished them happiness."

Cavaliere indeed drove them to Chengdu. They arrived in Chengdu on November 17, just a bit less than a month after they left it. The next day, Harkness and Su Lin boarded an airplane for Shanghai. Young trekked back to panda country.

CHAPTER TEN

PANDA-MONIUM

The propeller plane stopped to refuel in Chongqing and Hankow. Harkness marveled at the incredible speed she was making on her return trip to Shanghai. To her surprise, news of her catch had preceded her, and the American press was waiting for her at the airport.

Within days, the newspapers were filled with the bad-pun headline "Panda-monium," which self-amused newspaper editors have put on nearly every story about pandas ever since. On November 18, the *New York Times* reported that "The American woman explorer, Mrs. William H. Harkness, Jr., of New York City, arrived today from the Tibetan border with a live panda—a rare, bear-like animal."

She was no longer a joke or a dilettante, but an "American woman explorer," who had been led not by some "Chinaman," but by a Chinese explorer. *Times* editorial writers, however, worried over the semantics of the first dispatches. If Mrs. Harkness's animal were merely a "panda," meaning red panda, the giant panda's distant and diminutive relative, then this was no great find. But if it were a giant panda, well, that would be a

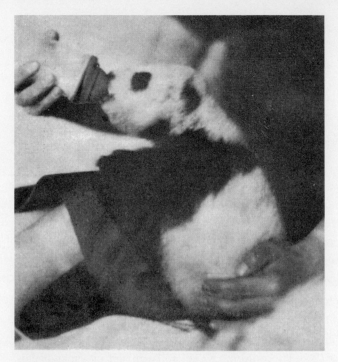

Bottle-feeding the baby panda. Courtesy China Journal.

panda of another color, rather akin to bringing home a unicorn or a Chinese dragon, as one writer put it.

Other than Arthur Sowerby, Harkness tried to avoid the Shanghai press for fear of stirring up the sleeping dragons of the Chinese government. How she managed to do so is puzzling, because she became close friends with the Shanghai correspondents from the two major New York newspapers, and she invited them to her room to talk and to play with the baby panda. But she seldom let go of her new prize, holding the panda close to her face, letting it nuzzle her hair and suck at her earlobes while she held forth to her new media friends.

Much of what she learned about pandas came from Sowerby, of course. (In her book, Harkness claims that Sowerby also told her of an Englishman's unsuccessful panda-hunting expedition which took place at the same time as hers—the mysterious rival expedition—but I could find no such reference in *China Journal*.) In fact, Harkness had suddenly become the world's expert on the species, and she talked like an expert in an exclusive interview for the *Times*.

"It was not altogether luck nor a premonition," she said. "Little is known about these queer and rare bears, but scientists have believed that they mate in April. Judging from the size of the adults, I thought their young would probably be born in October. This is the main reason I brought the milk bottle." [. . .]

"Just now this baby subsists entirely on warm Klim [a commercial brand of powdered milk in the era], to which, on the advice of Shanghai physicians, are added some proteins usually found in the milk of wild animals.

"The youngster weighs only a little more than four pounds, but has cost me about $5,000 a pound in American money," [. . .]

Harkness and her baby. From Ruth Harkness's collection,
courtesy of Mary Lobisco.

"I feed her only when she wakens and wails for food, instead of having a regular nursing schedule. And I have never subjected the little animal to artificial heat. I keep the radiators turned off and all the windows opened, regardless of temperature. The baby's basket, though, is lined with a thick woolen blanket and the inner nest is made of thick Turkish towels."

In her conversations with reporters, she always spoke highly of Quentin Young, often referred to in newspaper articles as the younger brother of Jack T. Young, the famous Chinese explorer of the Tibetan borderlands.

"Mrs. Harkness is loud in her praises of Quentin Young's kindness and efficiency in managing the expedition," according to one account, "and in token of her appreciation, she left with Quentin Young, as a present for his fiancee, her own wedding ring."

In her book she lets on how she pines for Young's company, especially in those moments when her Shanghai friends have left her alone to weep into her whiskey-soda. Despite what she wrote, her last two weeks in Shanghai were hardly inconspicuous. She visited nightclubs and attended cocktail parties until her voice gave out, often with Su Lin in tow. This hardly seems the best way to avoid the notice of the press.

The Eastman Kodak Company sent a photographer to shoot pictures of explorer and panda in their room at the Palace Hotel. Her own photographs—700 frames—had been ruined, she claimed, when a piece of film jammed the works, a klutzy misfortune that has fueled critics' suspicions that she never went to panda country at all.

One sees from the Kodak picture shoot, that Harkness was thinking ahead—to what's now called product placement. One shot shows Harkness bottle-feeding the tiny animal; but the

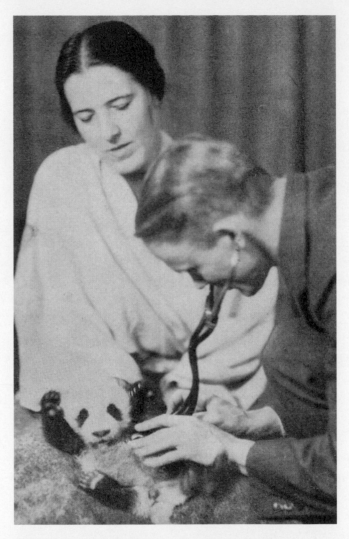

Harkness has a Shanghai pediatrician examine the panda cub.
Courtesy China Journal.

Harkness camped out in her Shanghai hotel room with the baby animal.
Courtesy China Journal.

photo's focus centers on the foreground where there was a carefully placed can of Klim powdered milk.

Her anthropomorphism is both amusing and endearing. She referred to the panda as "absurdly baby-like," and carried on as if it were a child. When she feared it was ill, she didn't call for a veterinarian, but for the best English-speaking pediatrician in Shanghai, who initially responded to her phone call by asking "What the devil is a baby pandor?" The good doctor, who joined the ranks of Harkness's new fast friends, prescribed an enema and a few drops of peppermint in water for the baby's colic, and suggested cod liver oil in the formula as well.

Despite advice to the contrary from those friends who knew China better than she, Harkness did consult with Chinese government officials about her giant panda, and she thought she'd get clear passage out of the country. But when she arrived at the docks with her entourage of friends and reporters near midnight on November 27, she was met by Chinese customs officials, who confiscated the panda.

Harkness was hysterical, by her account and those of others. The customs officials assured her that they'd give her a receipt for the animal, but Harkness was rightfully terrified that it would die if left alone in a shed at the docks like a piece of lost luggage. She'd proven her mettle in the wilds of Sichuan. In what may have been her bravest act in China, she stood up to the customs bureaucrats and insisted on staying by herself in the Customs shed, sitting up all night to feed and protect her "baby." Her ship sailed without her.

A friend came to relieve her in the morning so that she could return to the Palace Hotel for more milk and some means of warming it. Then she went back to the Customs shed and drank coffee and worried until her friends posted a bond for the animal. At eleven the next morning, she and the panda checked back into the Palace.

Over the next several days, Harkness's considerable Shanghai connections, including the Socony Oil executive, lobbied on her behalf. The New York papers speculated that Harkness would never be allowed to leave with the panda, but Sowerby knew better. As he later wrote, "To have tried to keep it in China would undoubtedly have ended in disaster and a great loss to scientific knowledge, for there is no institution in this country equipped to rear such a difficult animal to keep alive."

China was caught in an embarrassing pickle. Though they didn't want the only captured animal of such a rare and typically

Chinese species to leave the country in possession of a foreigner, if it were to die in their care—and likely it would—they would face international scorn and ridicule.

On December 1, 1936, government officials issued an export permit for a bit less than $50 US. Harkness still claimed she'd never obtained any sort of official permission to hunt pandas, and those claims may have complicated her stay. Nonetheless, the Chinese issued the permit for "One Dog," valued at $20.

Harkness boarded the ocean liner President McKinley the next day and locked herself in her cabin, lest anything else go wrong. In a way it did. Another American woman boarding ship with a poodle was confronted by Customs police who demanded to see the paperwork for the "panda" she was trying to sneak on board. The poor woman had no idea what a panda was, and somehow talked her way past the officials. This time Harkness set sail.

Meanwhile, Quentin Young raced back to his hunting camps above Zhaopo and searched furiously for pandas. He had considered capturing another alive—this time he'd use those big traps and cages he'd brought—but he was suddenly pressed for time. His girlfriend Diana had wired him from Shanghai, asking that he come back as soon as possible. Her mother had been ill, but Diana had put off traveling back home to Makassar, Celebes, in the Dutch East Indies, because she wanted to graduate from college, and because she was attending training camp and competing in track and field events with the hope of qualifying for the Chinese National team. Now her mother was dying, and she had to return, with Young or without him.

Young was afraid he'd lose her, so he rushed to finish his business—namely fulfilling Harkness's agreement to provide a panda for the Academia Sinica. At the same time, he'd received another cable, this one from Harkness, asking him to wait for her in Sichuan, because she wanted to return from America as soon as she delivered her panda.

He answered by cable, "December quit, back spring." She telegraphed for clarification, thinking he was making some arcane comment on the panda mating season. He meant that he was leaving as soon as possible. Within days he had shot a panda near the area where they'd captured Su Lin. He spotted it on a high rock ledge, and when he shot, the animal fell off the edge and crushed its skull in the fall. Young skinned it, but needed to keep hunting for a more perfect specimen. Even if the Great White Hunters had found pandas to be elusive, Young tracked a third within days and shot it.

In his photos from that hunt, instead of the scowl he wore while Harkness was there, he now had a huge smile. He'd bought a live red panda from local hunters and placed it on top of one of the dead giant pandas. Then he photographed himself smilingly pointing to both.

"Ah see? They don't know each other," he'd say later when he showed the photo to me.

Whereas it had taken five days to get Harkness back to Chengdu, Young traveled day and night and got there in two. Two weeks after Harkness's departure for America, Young arrived by steamer in Shanghai, as the city's daily English-language newspaper said, "in wake of the flurry of excitement which Shanghai was exhibiting a short while ago over Mrs. Ruth Harkness and her baby giant panda."

Quentin Young, in a photo that accompanied stories of the Ruth Harkness expedition. Courtesy China Journal.

The photograph of Young that Harkness gave to the press showed him smiling goofily while wearing the kind of flapped hat that aviators and tank troops wore, looking, essentially, like a foreigner. Young's interview in the Shanghai papers was illustrated with a photo of the thoroughly modern young man in a dark suit and a fashionable hair cut. The headline read "No More Pandas."

149

"When Mr. Quentin Young arrived in Shanghai yesterday after completing a rather eventful expedition in Szechwan," it continued, "he remarked that he is through with the business of giant panda hunting forever."

Indeed, he'd stashed the two panda pelts beneath his bed at school, never to see them again, because he never got back there.

Diana was still waiting in Shanghai. Her mother had already died, but her father had called her home. He had arranged a marriage for her, telling her that he could no longer wait, because he'd die of sorrow in a year and never live to see his daughter's wedding. So Young and Diana set sail for Makassar to thwart the arranged marriage. Of course, when they arrived there, Diana's father was scandalized that they'd traveled alone together and insisted that they marry immediately.

By the time they returned to China the next July, Diana was pregnant, and China had just plunged unwillingly into war with Japan. Young and his wife joined the rest of the family in Macao where they had taken refuge, and Young took a job in a Hong Kong bank. The baby, Jenny, was born in November 1937.

Ruth Harkness's ship docked in San Francisco on December 18. The press, of course, was waiting for her once again. The airlines clamored for the privilege of flying her and the panda home to New York, but Harkness thought she'd rather take a grand tour on the train. Besides, if she flew, she worried that she'd have to put her baby in a cold and unpressurized luggage compartment.

She missed the first train and had to take one the next day. Two days later, she stopped in Chicago to visit with officials from the Field Museum and the Chicago Zoological Society. There she met Edward Bean, director of the Brookfield Zoo and his son Robert, also a zoo official, and they tried to talk her into leaving Su Lin with them right then and there.

The press—and probably Harkness as well—had always assumed she'd bring the animal to the Bronx Zoo. Curiously, New York Zoological directors were already backing away, telling reporters that Mrs. Harkness had been out of touch with them. Speculation ran rampant as to how much a giant panda was worth. No less an expert than Arthur Sowerby scoffed at press reports that it might muster a price of $20,000. He thought the figure would be $5,000 to $10,000.

Harkness wanted $20,000. That's how much she claimed she had spent to obtain Su Lin. In short, she was broke. But she made it clear that she didn't really want to sell the panda. She was willing to give it to any qualified institute that would put up the money she needed to go back to China to find another. Through the press, the Bronx Zoo offered an insultingly low $2,000 for the panda, and the know-nothing press opined that it was a fair price for unseen goods.

Harkness arrived at Grand Central Station the very next day, December 23. Her family was there to greet her—and yet again, so was the press. They rushed off to the Algonquin Hotel—Harkness feared her apartment was too small for Su Lin, who now weighed ten pounds—and she made a show of raising all the windows and turning off the radiators in mid-winter Manhattan, again to simulate the cold Tibetan climate.

Jane Jones, Harkness's niece remembered "Dashing Aunt Ruth" arriving by taxicab at her family's house in Jamaica, Queens, then going through her ritual of opening all the windows to make the panda happy.

"I don't hold babies of any kind," Jones told me. She was a teenager at the time. "Oh my God, this was her baby!"

But on Christmas Eve, Harkness was again left all alone and crying into her drink, when one of her old roommates showed up at her hotel room door, and the three of them—Harkness, roommate, and panda—went out on the town.

There were parties to attend. Su Lin Young, the panda's namesake, remembers going with her husband Jack to a party in Harkness's honor. The Youngs—"China's only woman explorer" and the "famous Chinese explorer of the Tibetan borderlands"—were quite in the background, she told me, "and Quentin was quite forgotten."

Even the Great White Hunters came to call, first, the Roosevelt brothers, Theodore and Kermit, who'd been the first Westerners to shoot a panda. A director from the Chicago Zoological Society was in the room with them, lobbying on behalf of the Brookfield Zoo. One more reason to bring the panda to Chicago, he argued, was that if it died, it could be mounted and placed on display next to the specimens that the Roosevelts had brought back from China. Colonel Roosevelt allegedly huffed, "I'd as soon think of mounting my own son as I would this baby." Dean Sage also visited with Harkness and Su Lin; the panda he'd shot had just been put on display at the American Museum of Natural History. And so did Brooke Dolan of the Philadelphia museum that funded the expedition in which Ernst Schaefer shot his panda. Somehow after seeing Harkness's playful teddy bear, shooting a giant panda no longer seemed such a courageous feat.

Harkness was also asked to speak to the Explorers Club, the first woman to ever do so, though what the Explorers really wanted was to see the panda. Harkness obliged.

The two of them appeared in print ads together. "Famous Explorer Discovers Nerve-Bracing Breakfast," read an advertisement for Quaker Oats. After a cartoon-strip rendition of her accomplishment—including a frame in which she, and she alone, spies the tiny panda cub—there is a signed statement: "Ruth Harkness says: 'I happen to love a life of adventure. For years I've considered Quaker Oats a splendid breakfast for active people.'"

The Bronx Zoo refused to take Su Lin, ostensibly because veterinarians there thought it had rickets. Its back legs pointed inward, and at the time no one realized that panda legs are turned that way. One wonders if the mismatch between Harkness's financial expectations and the zoo's offer played into the decision. The animal already weighed 13 pounds and Harkness worried that it would soon be beyond her abilities to manage it.

The Brookfield Zoo, on the other hand, was aggressive and would take the risk. It still wanted the panda, and was willing to pay $14,000 and help arrange financing for Harkness's next adventure, according to George Speidel, who was captain of the guard at Brookfield. Harkness brought it there in February 1937, and Speidel became Su Lin's keeper.

"After she put it in our hands, she was kind of glad to be free of the responsibility," he told me. "It weighed 13 pounds when it came and got to weigh about 225 pounds or so. I remember it at that size getting up on my lap."

Speidel was also Harkness's keeper while she was in Chicago, and his duties included driving her between the downtown Stevens Hotel and the zoo, which is in the city's western suburbs.

Of course, nobody had any idea of how to take care of a baby giant panda, even at a world-class zoo. Director Bean's daughter

Mary was a licensed nurse, and at first she was put in charge of the baby's care. Mary Bean soon became Mrs. George Speidel. As Mr. Speidel said to me, "We call it our first child."

Su Lin's celebrity soon eclipsed Ruth Harkness's, drawing as many as 40,000 visitors on a weekend. John Barrymore the actor, Alexander Woolcott the writer, even Al Capone came to see Su Lin. Speidel says that Helen Keller stamped her feet with delight on meeting the giant panda.

"It got to be such a terrific animal then," Speidel said. "It was probably the most important animal to ever come to Brookfield."

And for good reason, judging from newsreels taken of the adolescent panda as it clowned with Robert Bean, grabbing his pants legs and then scurrying up trees. Mary and George Speidel both insisted that when Harkness returned for visits, Su Lin would perk up as soon as she saw her.

The animal graced the covers of magazines, with and without Harkness. Mary Speidel claims that she even fielded a call from Vaudeville producers who wanted her go on the road with the panda for $300 a month. The panda stayed home. But Ruth Harkness was soon back on the road.

CHAPTER ELEVEN

THE RAPE OF THE PANDA

One day after Harkness set sail, Floyd Tangier Smith was already accusing her of theft, and his complaint appeared in the *New York Times* under the headline "Charges Hunters Took Baby Panda by Deception.'"

"Floyd T. Smith, explorer and big game hunter and a partner of William H. Harkness, Jr., who died in Shanghai in February of this year, in a published statement, charges that Mrs. Harkness did not capture the baby panda with which she sailed for America yesterday.

"Mr. Smith alleges he has received word from Chaopo, Szechwan, [Zhaopo, Sichuan] his headquarters, that his hunters had located the mother panda three months ago and watched her build her nest. They knew the baby panda had been born, Mr. Smith said, and they were only waiting until the little panda had been nearly weaned, when they intended to attempt to capture both.

"Mr. Smith charges that Mrs. Harkness's hunters learned the location of the nest from his men and that her hunters walked up and took away the infant panda before its eyes were opened.

"He also declares he saw Mrs. Harkness before she started inland, and he asserts she then agreed not to enter the territory his men were working."

The accusation has persisted ever since.

"Whose territory?" Quentin Young shouted at me when I asked him about the charges. "This is Chinese territory and we are Chinese!"

It's curious that Smith felt so robbed. After all, he'd dismissed as impractical first Bill Harkness's and then Ruth Harkness's decisions to only hunt for pandas. When Quentin Young and Ruth Harkness proved the contrary, he obviously realized he was mistaken. And despite his reserved and formal protests to the press, he took the news hard, as evidenced in a February 17, 1937, letter to his usual confessor, Curator Simms at the Field Museum:

"I have just recently got out of the hospital once more," he began. "While I was in there a letter came from you which, I believe, merely asked me to hurry up with the lists for the specimens. At the time I was quite helpless.

"I have been living through a strange experience, which now seems like a long succession of nightmares with brief periods of wakening, but was actually characterized by fits of sudden loss of consciousness or by more frequent and prolonged periods of extreme physical and nervous exhaustion when I was quite conscious but unable to do anything at all.

"After being in the hands of a nerve specialist for many weeks without relief my own doctor called in a dentist and the x-ray revealed a condition of infected teeth that had been pouring large doses of poison into my system for a long time.

"The teeth have been removed and I am now steadily gaining back lost strength and weight. But what had made matters very much worse, by that time, was the cumulative effect of long continued periodic nerve strain due to many anxieties and worries that began with my inability to take to America some $15,000 worth of birds and animals that I had brought to Shanghai two years ago; followed by harrowing mental experiences during the wasted year when the two disappearances and several illnesses of Mr. Harkness finally resulted in his death, and culminating in the later activities of Mrs. Harkness when she, practically, stole a giant panda out of the central collecting camp that I had established at Chaopo, two and a half days journey from Chengtu."

Apparently he was overcome at this point and had to get up from his typewriter for several days. The letter continues:

"The above is as far as I had got in a letter to you dated February 5th, since when I have again suffered a nervous collapse that kept me in bed for four days and has left me still rather completely groggy.

"I had intended to tell you something more of how Mrs. Harkness got the panda. I can not do that further than to say that the story of its capture is pure bunk designed to hide the fact that she bought it in my camp, contrary to her promise not to go there since she did not travel ten days from Chengtu; she did not establish any collecting camps of her own; she was not inspecting traps when the panda was found and had not set a single trap for the catching of pandas; but she did go direct from Chengtu to Chaopo when she learned that a panda had already been captured there and bought it from men that I have been paying for the last four years who were holding it for delivery to me when it might be possible for me to return to Szechwan and take delivery of the 40 or more head of birds and animals that they now have there for me. Thank God that she did not take away anything else.

"I cannot write anything more now. When I can I will tell you something more of this rather interesting story of the 'rape' of the panda."

Young certainly *did* have photographs of his panda camps and photographs of the two pandas he shot. What he did not have were any photographs that unmistakably show Harkness in panda country.

Of course Smith's accusatory letter to the Field Museum bears a striking resemblance to the one he wrote to the California pheasant collector in 1935, when Jack and Quentin Young scooped him by bringing pheasants to a rival collector. Then, too, Smith had railed that the Youngs had taken advantage of his experience and his hunters and his good graces.

Still, Smith stuck with his accusations, reiterating them in a BBC radio show later that year. He wrote letter after letter, claiming that one of his hunters, a man named Kuoh, had sold the questionable panda to Harkness.

It's hard to say whether Smith invented the story himself to save face—or if his hunters were saving face by inventing a story to cover their own ineptitude. Whatever the case, Smith likely *wanted* to believe it: How else could an inexperienced woman and a boy "Chinaman" have achieved what he, with all his great prestige and experience, could not? At least not yet.

That sexist and racist prejudice was so strong that rumors persist to this day, some of them quite fantastic. For example, there are printed stories asserting that Smith and Bill Harkness found a panda early on, but it died, and so they went off to the Philippines together to hunt some other species. That Ruth

Harkness bought her panda from missionaries, or that she bought it in a tea shop in Guanxian from hunters who were delivering it to Smith.

Then, Smith claimed, Harkness slunk around Shanghai mostly to avoid his discovering that she'd stolen his panda. He even claimed that she'd explained to him personally that she had bought it from hunters.

In 1965, Gerald Russell, the Englishman who had briefly teamed up with Smith and Bill Harkness, wrote letters to an attorney in Atlanta, repeating the charge that Harkness had bought the panda cub from a local hunter.

And George Schaller heard similar stories from his Chinese colleagues at the Wolong panda preserves maintained near Zhaopo by the Chinese government. One of the scientists there had allegedly talked to a hunter who told him that Harkness had bought the panda. Schaller asked if he could speak to that particular hunter, and he was told that such a conversation would be a very difficult thing to obtain. And that was that.

"Has Quentin Young given you an honest answer about that panda?" Schaller asked me when we first met in 1990.

Of course, no one dared ask such questions of Jack Young when he visited Wolong in the late 1980s. Instead, local residents told him they remembered him, or remembered his brother, Wolong being just a few valleys away from Zhaopo. Such is the shifting, malleable nature of Chinese realities.

The question continued to plague Quentin Young.

"If I lie, do I gain anything?" he said more than once.

And if local hunters had offered them a panda they'd captured, Young and Harkness would certainly have bought it. Their object was to "obtain" a panda, not to capture it personally.

The Young brothers bought animals all the time, and so did all of the rest of the collectors, including Smith. In fact, if Smith had been the first to obtain a panda, he himself would have bought it from local hunters. Within a few months, he did just that—and no one accused him of anything. Which is another bone of contention for Quentin Young.

In December 1983, *Smithsonian* magazine published a story about the Smith-Harkness debate, without talking to the remaining eye witnesses, or for that matter, knowing if they still existed. Young wrote a precise and controlled letter of protest, a portion of which was published in the letters column at the front of the magazine.

"There *is* an answer to your panda question," it began.

"Tangier Smith, as you say, was an 'old China hand.' That carried some virtues and a great many limitations. Smith either out of ignorance of panda characteristics or out of a sense of 'old China hand' melodrama made far more of the panda situation than necessary.

"Pandas are shy creatures. Like any wild animal, they can have their moments of ferocity, but they are basically a docile animal even in the wild. Local people in panda country do not run from them, and in that time a half century ago, if a panda wandered into human territory it would gaze at these strange upright folk and then lumber off into the protection of bamboo.

"Smith must not be diminished, for as you say, his knowledge of animal care and taxidermy, and his reputation with the government and institutions were excellent. The fact is that no professionals and certainly no westerners of that time knew very much about panda behavior.

" 'Old China hand[s]' in general did not trouble themselves with learning the Chinese language. Chinese for their part have always considered the foreigner exploitable. These two points create an enormous gulf. Add to this an entrepreneurial sense that is almost synonymous with being Chinese and you have a situation where perhaps Smith was the game, the 'fair game,' in the eyes of the mountain people. In typical Chinese fashion they performed according to his expectations. He thought the capture of pandas should be difficult, so they allowed him to think so.

"Enter Ruth Harkness: she had a great asset. Quentin Young. The Young family cannot be dismissed simply as 'guides.' Jack Young was perhaps China's most qualified naturalist of the time. His younger brother revered him.

As the letter went on, Young continued to refer to himself in the third person: "Quentin was an educated young man," it read. "He was fluent in English, his native Cantonese, Mandarin, Shanghai and Szechwan dialects. Ruth Harkness in her book *The Lady and the Panda* comments on the qualities of his youthful personality. Apparently, the winsome qualities were appealing to his own people, the Chinese. Certainly, with him they were willing to chuckle and shrug their shoulders and say, 'Go out there and find a bei-shung. It's not hard. These are the indications you look for. Quentin did just that. Admittedly, it was an extraordinary piece of good fortune that Quentin heard that tiny whimper. However, it certainly was not the big game he sought on this, his grand adventure away from the shadow of his brother Jack. There is no way as a matter of his personal character or his pride, that the 22 year old would have contrived to have this minuscule animal be the end result of all his effort. In fact, it was humiliating to him to find out both that Ruth Harkness was satisfied with this infant creature and prepared for it with baby goods.

"Your article ends on the note, 'Although none of the principal characters in the sag[a] of Su Lin enjoyed a happy ending, . . .' but you are wrong. THE principal character in that little drama has not come to his end. Though he may not be as 'winsome' now as he was then, nor at this time agree with these flowery estimates kindly offered, Quentin Young, now 70, is very much alive.

"I am he.

"If, unknown to me, Mrs. Harkness cut up China with Smith and made a 'hands-off' arrangement for the Min area, then it is only a further statement of the arrogant attitude of foreigners of the time toward China. It was the custom among nations and individuals to lay out a grid over the vastness of China for their own territories. China was CHINA, and I, Chinese. Smith indicated that he had an elaborate system in his anger over the Harkness coup. We used nothing of Smith's; nor did we need it. We simply needed a Chinese passing through his own country. I happened to be that Chinese. In fact, all that entourage and the Western woman were an encumbrance. My later life proved this as I brought down from Szechwan pandas for museums and now to my great sorrow innumerable pelts. With regard to this latter matter, you have made me proud to think that perhaps this one small act in my life has been a rallying point for the preservation of not only pandas, but of all the endangered species. You see, we *all* acted out of some degree of ignorance.

"My brother, Jack, also still living, did more than accompany the Roosevelts. Both of us have contributed specimens to zoos hidden behind the names of those who provided funds, as well as to museums such as the Field Museum in Chicago where I have walked, [in] some cases remembering these creatures in the last moments of their lives . . . "

For emphasis, he sent photographs of his panda camp, of his dead pandas, and of himself visiting with the mounted remains of Su Lin at the Field Museum, though the magazine did not publish them.

Young and Harkness did prove to the world that pandas were not ferocious killers and that capturing them was not difficult. And so it was open season on pandas. In short order, the old China hand, Floyd "Ajax" Smith, had his own. And he did not find them himself, though no one seemed to care.

In June 1937, Smith's hunters captured two subadult giant pandas in the mountains northwest of Chengdu. At first he kept them in a garden at West China Union University in Chengdu and talked of possibly breeding them, but then decided to take them to Europe to sell them.

One of them, a 400-pound specimen, had contracted a blood infection from a foot wound caused by a trap, and it died en route to Chongqing. The second weighed 200 pounds. And though Smith had let the world know he'd caught his own pandas, he had dyed this one brown to get it to Shanghai beneath the gaze of any meddling rural authorities. Jack Young told me he saw the dyed bear in Shanghai.

Smith named it Jenny, and it was as tame and charming as a pet. Smith posed for photographs while lying on the ground next to the panda, scratching its head, and standing above the animal, which he held on a leash, as if he were walking a big black-and-white dog.

In July 1937, he loaded it onto a freighter bound for Europe. He'd shaved its fur, hoping it could better withstand the summer heat, but, tragically, Jenny died before the ship reached Singapore. Smith speculated that if the heat hadn't killed it, then its diet had.

*Floyd T. Smith in Shanghai with the first of the giant
pandas he captured. The animal died en route to Europe.
Courtesy* China Journal.

*   *   *

A month later, Ruth Harkness was back in Shanghai to find a mate for Su Lin. As she later wrote, she "arrived simultaneously with the Japanese." On July 7, Chinese and Japanese troops fired at each other across the Marco Polo Bridge outside Beijing and the two countries were at war.

Harkness reached Shanghai on August 12 and checked into the Palace Hotel. Two days later the hotel was bombed, though Harkness was not there when it happened. She met with Arthur Sowerby while she was in town, and she brought him pictures of Su Lin at the Brookfield Zoo. Sowerby mentioned the photos in his next column, but apologized to his readers for not printing them and promised to run them in a future issue, "the present one being rather crowded out with Shanghai war pictures."

And indeed it was, horrible photos of shattered bodies scattered on sidewalks and in marketplaces. Because of the war, Harkness had to take the roundabout route to Chengdu, south to Hanoi, in what was then Indochina, by train back to Yunnan, China, and then north to Chengdu.

Sowerby reported that she was supposed to meet up with Quentin Young somewhere in South China, but it didn't happen, and Harkness made her way alone, relying on the contacts she and Young had made the year before.

She spent the winter in the castle at Zhaopo with Wang, the fat cook from the earlier expedition as her major domo, a period she later described in an article in *Gourmet* magazine as "the winter in which I ate an estimated ten thousand dollars' worth of rare pheasants." Essentially, Wang was cooking for her the same prized birds that Smith and the Young brothers had been trying to transport to the United States just a few years before. In December, the hunters she'd hired trapped two young pandas for her. One died shortly afterwards, but she took the other and headed home.

On the way back out of the country she was held up in Hankow while the Japanese bombed that city. Her niece Jane Jones told me that Harkness came face to face with the war in Hankow and ran into an alley to vomit when she saw the corpses in the street. Finally she flew the surviving panda to Hong Kong to even greater fanfare than the first had garnered. This time, the newsreel cameras were waiting for her when she stepped off the plane, wearing a spotted fur coat and fighting back a funny frown as she struggled to contain a squirming, scratching, nipping panda cub.

Quentin Young met her in Hong Kong, and he appears in the newsreel in his dark, banker's suit, a black Vitalis lock of hair bouncing over his forehead as he plays with the animal. Lowell Thomas, the newsreel narrator, doesn't seem to notice him, however, ecstatic in his praise for the intrepid Mrs. Harkness. In the last scene of the clip, Harkness whisks up her living teddy bear and strides confidently up the gangway of a propeller-driven airliner that took her directly to Seattle.

The newsreel didn't show the soap opera playing behind the scenes. Harkness had named the new panda Diana, after Young's wife. She asked if she could be godfather to Young's daughter, but Young refused. And she tried to convince Young to come visit her in New York, under auspices of giving lectures. She truly and unselfishly was willing to share the limelight with Young. But he refused to come unless Harkness also paid passage for his wife and daughter, which she could ill afford.

Harkness introducing the pandas to each other at the Brookfield Zoo.
© Chicago Tribune. *All rights reserved. Used with permission.*

Harkness brought this second panda to the Brookfield Zoo in February, 1938, and was paid a price close to the one she'd received for Su Lin. Zoo officials changed its name to the more appropriate sounding Chinese name, Mei Mei, which means "little sister." The photographs of Harkness introducing Mei Mei to Su Lin are priceless, two black-and-white fluff balls touching noses. Su Lin clearly still remembered her captor as a surrogate mom, and photographers captured the two of them rolling in the snow in a playful embrace.

A few months later on April 1, 1938, Su Lin was dead. She'd apparently choked on a twig, though an autopsy later determined that she'd died of pneumonia. It also determined that "she" was a "he." Harkness mourned bitterly, and so did all of Chicago. And then, the corpse of the most famous animal in the world went to the Field Museum, where, contrary to Colonel Roosevelt's admonition, it was mounted and put on display. It's still there today, and until recently bore no particular explanatory plaques other than a tiny brass plate that said, "Su Lin, courtesy of the Brookfield Zoo." Now it sits in an elegant glass case next to a perpetually looped videotape of when it romped playfully at the Brookfield Zoo.

By the time Harkness left her new panda in Chicago, Floyd Smith was back in Chengdu, taking charge of a new batch of pandas. A German animal dealer named Otto Fockelmann, claimed that Smith had told him that missionaries had noticed that a group of six pandas regularly came to bathe in a pond near the mission. The missionaries had built walls around the pond, leaving two openings for the pandas to enter, Fockelmann said, and once they were inside, they blocked them off, trapping all six animals inside. And then the missionaries reportedly contacted Smith to come get them.

Chris Catton is a British documentarian who has filmed and written a book about giant pandas.

"As a zoologist, the one bit of the Fockelmann stuff that I can be sure is complete nonsense, is the watering hole business. Pandas have absolutely no need to visit a regular watering hole— this is not the Namib Desert!" he wrote to me in an e-mail. "There is a lot of water in their diet, and the whole of their range is sodden most of the time, with lots of streams and rivers. It's cold, and pandas are on a tight energy budget. The water is near freezing (mostly snow melt) and bathing in it would quickly lower their temperature. I've never found any evidence of them bathing or playing in water."

Nonetheless, Smith had obtained six giant pandas. And though Smith was gravely ill with tuberculosis, he managed to come up to Chengdu to arrange for their shipment to Shanghai. Judging from telegrams I found with the New York Zoological Society, one of them was earmarked for the Bronx Zoo. The zoo had reiterated its standing offer of $2,500. Smith politely told zoo officials that the offer was very low, but that he'd be willing to deal if he could lock up film rights for the comical animals. Somehow the deal never happened.

And though the press reported in April that the pandas were on their way out of western China, Smith had only gotten them as far as Chongqing. He'd expected to fly them to Hong Kong, but he couldn't get their cages through the airplane hatches and was forced to take them back to Chengdu instead. There he kept them staked and chained in the front lawns of European friends living in Chengdu.

Finally, in October, he'd found a pair of trucks headed east, and hired the truck drivers to take his pandas along with a shipment of heavy machinery. He himself was far too sick to accompany the trip, and so he sent his wife Elizabeth while he flew back to Hong Kong to finalize arrangements.

It was a horrible trip. They were forced to detour weeks out of the way to travel around the war. A few days out of Chongqing, one of the trucks rolled down an embankment, killing one of the pandas. They drove on to South China, and loaded the remaining five pandas aboard a small ship and sailed for Kowloon.

In November, Smith and the pandas shipped out again for Europe and arrived in London on Christmas Eve. There, a happy but exhausted-looking Smith and one of the pandas posed for photographs for *Time* Magazine. Of those five animals, one died shortly after reaching England. Three went to the London Zoo, and the fifth was leased to Fockelmann, who took it on tour through Europe and eventually delivered it to the St. Louis Zoo.

Smith, however, was near his end. He checked into the hospital for the final stages of his tuberculosis, though his wife managed to get him back to the Smith family home on Long Island, where he died on July 13, 1939. He was 58 years old, and he never let go of his contention that Ruth Harkness had stolen his glory and his first panda.

If the western world was ecstatic about seeing pandas in zoos, wiser men were already worrying about how easily hunters were hauling them out of their Tibetan lairs. In May, 1938, Arthur Sowerby pondered just that, once again under the heading "The Lure of the Giant Panda."

"It will be seen from the foregoing that the lure of the giant panda is a very real thing," he wrote. "The rarity of the animal, its elusiveness, the mystery surrounding its habits, the anomalous nature of its diet (in a wild state it eats nothing but bamboo), its remarkable appearance—all have contributed their share toward making it one of the most sought-after animals in the world to-day. The only danger is that the desire on the part of the natural history museums of Europe and America to possess specimens, or the mania for trophies on the part of sportsmen may lead to the over-hunting of the giant panda and its possible extermination. At present the species enjoys no form of protection other than that afforded by the inaccessibility of the country in which it lives."

By August of 1938, even before Ajax Smith had gotten his new pandas out of Chengdu, Ruth Harkness had come and gone on her third panda-hunting expedition. She'd contracted with Quentin Young again, but he'd insisted she stay home in America until he called for her. On his way to Chengdu, he stopped in Hankow to visit with his brother Jack, who had enlisted in the War Area Service Corps, a branch of the Chinese Army that served as a liaison between General Chiang Kaishek and the foreign militaries. Jack was a colonel already, "A bigger shot than I was, always," as Quentin Young remembered. But Quentin was inspired to enlist as well, and he headed up to Chengdu in his new blue uniform.

Before he got there, however, he took off the epaulets and put on a civilian hat, so that he wouldn't look like a Nationalist soldier. Sichuan, after all, was still full of Communist sympathizers, including, perhaps, some of the companions with whom Young planned to hunt.

Almost immediately, the men he hired in Zhaopo caught two pandas for him, and he cabled Harkness to come retrieve them. She had planned to take the slow route through Europe, then India to Burma and Yunnan. Instead she booked air passage and arrived in Chengdu in the remarkable time of eight days. There was only one panda left when she got there.

Young had brought the larger of the two to Chengdu and kept it in a cage in the courtyard of Cavaliere's mansion. It seemed tame enough, and Young has photographs of the animal sniffing in and out of its cage. But one night during a violent thunderstorm, it went berserk and smashed its cage and then started tearing its way into the house, threatening the occupants.

"It tried to find a way out," Young told me. "I tried to corner him again, but what can you do in such weather? He was furious."

His voice cracked when he told the rest: "I . . . I shot it."

That made Young the only man to ever shoot three pandas, a distinction that has never made him proud. But the incident also pointed out a new facet of panda behavior, that although they seemed docile most of the time, they were still capable of a dangerous ferocity.

Harkness arrived too late. When she saw Young in uniform, she took him to task for joining the Army. He was already beyond patience.

"What is it with you Americans?" he screamed at her. "You let China be invaded. And people get killed. Yet you're spending money on pandas!"

He'd left the other panda, a cub, in a woodshed in Zhaopo, and he told Harkness that if she wanted it, she'd have to go there herself to get it. This time, he was really through with the business of hunting pandas.

Harkness dutifully trekked up to the mountains. She named this cub Su-Sen, but it was unlike the others. It didn't like humans—or her. In fact, it wouldn't tolerate her. As she put it, she had nothing to show but scratches and bruises for all her troubles, and it broke her heart.

"So the expedition was put in reverse," she wrote in the foreword to her second book, *Pangoan Diary*, "and with Wang, my cook, we traveled back, up over the old caravan route that has changed little since the time of Christ, and plunged into the bamboo-jungled wilderness to leave Su-Sen at the exact spot where she had been captured. There we lived in a cave for a week, lingering to see if she would come back for the food to which we had accustomed her.

"After days and nights of extreme discomfort—even misery, for I was ill—she did come back, but it was by mistake. The little black-and-white furry youngster looked just once at civilization in the form of Wang and me and ran as if all the demons of hell were at her heels. Then it was that I wondered why anyone ever left the town in which she was born to seek out the unknown in the forests and jungles far from all familiar things. I vowed then that I would return to my own land and perhaps again design fashionable and ugly clothes to be sold in smart shops."

When Harkness left China, she told Sowerby that she still might return for yet another panda, this time to take it on tour to benefit Chinese war refugees. Perhaps Young's angry words had hit their target. She never made good on her threat to return to clothing design. And except for the books she wrote, Harkness was out of the panda business, too.

On her way home to New York in 1939, she took a detour in India and voyaged to the Eastern Himalayas. She wrote a letter to the *China Journal* from there that March, noting that she'd seen the naturalist and fellow panda hunter Ernst Schaefer there. Next stop, Liverpool, England, where according to a messily typed bio I got from her sister, she left with "one vaguely Persian cat bought in Liverpool for two shillings and sixpence: Lady Jennifer."

But there were more live giant pandas taken out of China in the next few years. Dean Sage arranged for one for the Bronx Zoo in May of 1939, and later that same year, a daily newspaper columnist from Chicago obtained one more for the Brookfield Zoo.

That was the last one. The Chinese government finally clamped down on panda exports. As Sowerby wrote in November, 1939, "... ruthless hunting for the rare animal resulted in a campaign by well known authorities on the giant panda to restrict the hunting and export of the animal in order to save it from extinction." And by then the war was burning so hot that Westerners had to start worrying about other matters.

CHAPTER TWELVE

WAR AND RUTH'S PEACE

Even before he left for Nanda Devi, Jack Young was already trying to drum up financing for his next collecting expedition in western China. It didn't matter one bit that the *New York Times* had referred to him as a famous explorer of the Tibetan borderlands. He was still a no-name "Oriental" to the museum curators. But when his brother Quentin returned from his first successful panda hunting expedition, Jack Young added that association into his sales pitch and landed his first and last commission for collecting.

The Field Museum had paid the Roosevelt brothers $20,000 apiece. The American Museum of Natural History offered Young $2,700, all the while reminding him that this was a great honor for a beginner like himself.

At about the same time, he'd contacted the Bronx Zoo because hunters he knew up near Minya Konka had captured a baby takin and were holding it for his arrival. He reminded the zoo officials of the two Tibetan bear cubs he'd delivered a year or so earlier, just so they'd remember how reliable he was.

The zoo offered him $1,200 for the takin, $2,000 if he could bring back two, a price disparity that Young protested. But unfortunately, before he could collect even the one animal, it had been torn apart and killed by a pack of dogs in the village where it had been tied up.

He'd planned to be in the field by March of 1937, but he was sidelined by an acute appendicitis. He'd also been in touch with several other museums to see if he could double up on fees and better cover his expenses, maybe even turn a small profit. But back in the States, the museum directors were apparently a tight and gossipy group, because more than one contacted the American Museum to let them know that Young was double dipping.

The American Museum curator was furious and scolded Young in a letter that began "I have been somewhat disturbed by the fact that you have written to several museums offering to dispose of material to be collected on your forthcoming expedition."

Jack Young apologized profusely and wrote embarrassed letters to the other museums withdrawing his offers. Then a bigger obstacle kept him out of the field—the Japanese invasion. The museum curators were getting concerned about their investment when they couldn't get hold of Young.

In August, they finally heard from him, and he was apologizing again. "You must also forgive me for the long stretch of silence," he wrote. "I was in Chengtu on the first stage of the journey to the interior when war broke out in Peking [Beijing] last month and I hurried back by plane in an effort to evacuate my family. That was impossible as all communications with the outside world were either blocked or destroyed by the Japanese. I barely managed to slip through the firing lines last week to get here, but all is not too well in Shanghai. I never saw such horrors."

He still needed to rescue his wife and new baby in Beijing, he continued, and he wasn't sure if he'd be able to recover his hunting guns from there, given Japanese restrictions. He hoped to ship his family off to New York and then head up to Chengdu, where he could be reached in care of Cavaliere, the customs commissioner.

But he never made it, because he was drafted into the Chinese Army and assigned to the War Area Service Corps. Theoretically, he was only obligated to six months of service, after which, he was optimistic he could return to his expedition. In May of 1938, he wrote to the museum on military letterhead, explaining that he would be bringing his family home to China in October and would proceed to Chengdu at that time. In the meantime, his brother Quentin had managed to shoot—or otherwise collect—a golden monkey carcass while on his last panda hunt. Jack Young was sending that to New York in the care of an American filmmaker who had been in China shooting war footage.

But apparently war and military service were not good enough excuses, because the museum curator began writing alarmed letters to Su Lin Young, Jack's wife, who was staying in New York. In a letter of her own in late May, she tried to explain Jack's predicament.

"Though I have not heard very frequently from my husband since my arrival in America," she wrote, "several of his letters have reached me by Clipper airmail. Jack has pledged six months service to the Chinese Military Affairs Commission and has been in Hankow since the seat of the Chinese Government was removed from Nanking [Nanjiang] to that city; the six months however, seemed to have stretched out to seven months. At present I believe he is in North China on an inspection tour of the fronts. Possibly you saw a mention of his name in the American newspapers after the Chinese victory at Taierzhuang.

He accompanied Captain [Evans] Carlson of the American Embassy to the scene of the battle to confirm reports of the Chinese victory."

She reiterated that her husband's collectors were hard at work, even if Jack was otherwise disposed.

"I am afraid I cannot furnish you any more information than this about Jack's whereabouts, but I am sure that you will hear from him directly in the near future. I do not know definitely when I shall be leaving for China as I am waiting for further word from him. The situation in China is so unsettled at present that it is hard to judge one's plans by it. Fortunately, I have a small daughter to keep me company during these long months of separation. I shall get in touch with you as soon as I hear from Jack."

But apparently that explanation was not adequate, either, because Su Lin Young was apparently called in for an interview with the curator in which she was berated on Jack's behalf. And somehow, judging from her next letter, she was the one making apologies.

"I must apologize for my foolish outburst yesterday," she wrote. "It was as embarrassing to me as it was to you, and made our interview an extremely uncomfortable one. I do not usually give way to my feelings so readily—but the months of mental strain, the thought of leaving my baby, the gruesome picture of my husband dying in the field—all of these caused me to lose control of myself for the moment. In taking personal affront to many things brought up in yesterday's conversation, I was perhaps being over sensitive.

"I am trying to look at the situation from your point of view," she said later in the letter. But she didn't have a lot of control over her husband's situation. And neither did he. War or no war, $2,700 must have been a lot of money. But Jack Young was going to be busy for quite a while.

Quentin Young has always been mysterious and evasive about how he spent the war years. It was never entirely clear to me whether or not he was in the Chinese Army, or whether his vagueness was intended to cover up things he did or things he didn't do and felt he should have.

"There are other ways to serve," he told me. "Ways to use your brain."

He had said he'd joined up with Jack's unit, but then apparently traveled quite freely about Asia for someone who was supposed to be in the military. He claims he wore a uniform when it served his purposes, then took it off if he was traveling through Communist-held territory. And, he claims, he had friends in both camps, including a young Communist associate who helped him on his last panda hunt.

He claimed he was a freelance spy: "A asks me to watch B, B asks me to watch C, C asks me to watch A," he told me. "The young people, they want to try every side and see which is the right party to choose. So sometimes I work for one or the other, but basically everyone has the same aim, which was to fight the Japanese."

He claimed he was perfect for the job: quiet, acquiescent, cooperative, nonconfrontational, fiercely patriotic, "kind of goofy looking."

But he always played cat and mouse with me as to what the job was.

"I also had a title," he once exclaimed.

What was it?

"I won't tell you!"

Until the war, his life story and his brother's were intertwined and easy to track. From the war on, their trails disappear, sometimes completely, and I had to rely heavily on what they told me. In 1939, however, Quentin Young turned up in Rangoon, attached to the Denis-Roosevelt Asiatic Expedition, ostensibly as a guide and interpreter, though he told me he had been sent as a censor by the Chinese government.

The expedition leaders, Armand Denis and his wife, Leila Roosevelt, a cousin of both presidents, were filmmakers specializing in exotic travel. In this case, they were shooting a pair of films that would be titled "East of Bombay" and "Wheels Across India."

As filmmakers, the Denises purportedly chronicled foreign oddities, in the vein of "Mondo Cane." In reality, they made Jurassic infomercials underwritten by the makers of Dodge trucks and automobiles. They rode to the edges of the earth in their faithful Dodges, rugged and ready trucks that could navigate anything the Third World could dish out. (Denis continued making films with subsequent wives.)

Quentin Young had been engaged for a proposed trek up the Burma Road, the Allies' backdoor route for bringing badly needed munitions to the Chinese war effort—what effort there was, anyway, as Chiang spent more time worrying about the Communists, who were supposed to be his allies, than he spent worrying about the Japanese.

The Denises wanted to film the Asian war. Along for the ride was an American travel writer named Hassoldt Davis, who produced a couple of books about the expedition's travels through Burma, China, and Nepal. The Nepal leg became a separate book; the Burma Road episode was included in a book called *The Land of the Eye*.

True to the genre, the book is written in that same old breezy American travelogue style that suggested that any hardship could be overcome with a little casual Yankee ingenuity. While Ruth Harkness's prose was merely jaunty, Davis's was downright arrogant, and he wisecracked about the most shocking of sights, for example, a child who "rumbled loosely from a fourth-story window." The following lines were even more heartless: to clean up the resultant mess, "two men labored for half and hour swabbing him from the sidewalk." One supposes that Denis' cameras kept running throughout. And while Harkness had fallen in love with everything about China, Davis kept a cynical distance.

The expedition visited a snake-infested temple where a woman enticed a king cobra from its lair and then kissed it on the mouth as it poised to strike. It filmed wild elephants and monsoons. Along the way Davis and friends uncovered some bizarre Asian rituals that seem less bizarre today: bodies covered by tattoos, Thai-boxing prize fights, and a game that sounds an awful lot like hacky sack.

Not surprisingly, the Chinese balked at allowing the expedition past its borders—which outraged the Americans. They were certain their film would help the Chinese garner support from the outside world, though Chiang wanted American support of a more substantial military sort. Quentin Young appears in the book in his role as guide, but Davis uses him as a foil for his own American condescension.

"Our Chinese interpreter and guide, Quentin Young, who had known many of the official Chinese intimately during his panda hunts, was unable to understand why his country, so eager for foreign sympathy, should first accept and then deny an expedition that could be relied upon, because of the proven sympathy and probity of each of its members, to produce a film record of China at war that should be a powerful influence for help abroad," Davis wrote. "Quentin held his lean, sensitive face in his hands.

" 'We are confused,' he groaned. 'We are so confused.'"

Terribly confused, evidently, not to realize that a film made to aggrandize American egos while advertising an American corporation, wouldn't be just what the Chinese Army needed.

Actually, Young would not have been of much help as either interpreter or guide, since he didn't speak the local dialects of Burma and wasn't at all familiar with that part of China. He claims he was there on behalf of the War Area Service Corps, keeping an eye on *The Land of the Eye*. The Chinese government had also sent troops as an escort.

In the end, the Americans were allowed to drive the road, but they were forbidden to film anything. And although Davis vehemently denies it, Young says they did film. He rode one of the trucks on a roof-mounted platform with a hand-held camera to capture everything the newsreel cameras did.

The expedition only made it a few days into China because the road had been hopelessly blocked by landslides. Before they departed, however, Young became the foil in another scene of the book that was made up of equal portions of scenes from John Wayne and Stepin Fechit movies. Young is youthful, philosophical, sensitive, enthusiastic to the point of rambling—unlike those two-fisted American men of few words.

"Quentin and Jack [the expedition's mechanic] in the tent next to us talked drowsily," Davis wrote. "Quentin was explaining China's New Life Movement. Jack grunted. China, said Quentin, had been a land of old men until now, of passive old men worshipping their passive ancestors, until the current war with Japan. Now the youth of China was taking over, and it was their intention, he asserted, that the war should continue for at least ten years longer, no matter what the cost in ceded territories. Jack's reply was half grunt, half snore. For only thus, said Quentin sleepily, could China be unified. The provinces were so separated, geographically and culturally, that the peasants of Shansi in the north, for example, had never realized that those of Yunnan, where we were camping now, were their racial brothers. The war was waking them gradually to their common danger, and there would be a unified China in time, if they could protract the war . . .

" 'Huh?' Jack mumbled, rousing.

"Quentin's voice tapered into silence. Roy turned on his cot beside mine. 'Hmmm, quite . . . ' he said. The expedition went to sleep.

"I spun awake through a dream to realize that the camp was a yowling bedlam. Something lunged against the tent and bent the supporting rod across my feet. Armand was shouting through the yowls, 'Dave! Roy! Jack!' The gentle Roy, the ant-feeder and baiter of lions, was already on his feet, and beyond him through the mosquito net flap I could see the silhouette of a man, legs wide apart, a gleaming *dah* swinging murderously in the rain-speckled beam of someone's flashlight. Two other black figures went hurtling past, Kachin bandits, all right, and not afraid of ghosts, either. There was no sound from the truck where our Black Guard cowered.

Jack Young (right) with Chiang Kaishek during World War II.
Courtesy June Young.

"I reached for my .38 and dropped it again. I might kill somebody. I slipped on the faithful brass knuckles that had seen me through a variety of troubles in the South Seas, but Roy pulled me back. He was calmly lighting one of the long magnesium flares we used for night photography. He began to wail as he zipped open the mosquito net. Then he bounded through it, howling like a banshee, and waving a blaze of light, rushed straight for the three bedraggled bandits. We all yelled and converged behind him. There was no hesitation on the bandits' part. They tumbled over each other toward the flooded rice fields. They went knee-deep into the ooze, lurching for a foothold. Leila flung a tin of baked beans after them and Roy flung the torch. We stood in the muck and laughed. The last laugh in China was ours."

Indeed. Even the American woman gets in on the laugh. But where was Quentin Young, the intrepid spy and big game hunter? Why would Davis even notice?—unless he needed someone to polish his faithful brass knuckles. It's unimaginable that a man as brave as Quentin Young would *not* have participated in the adventure; he was no stranger to gunplay and Asian bandits. But Davis's tale was obviously too all-American for him to have noticed.

After returning from Rangoon, Young told me in his most mysterious voice, that he traveled to Haiphong and Saigon to measure the loyalties of the Chinese populations there. And in 1941, with the imminent fall of Hong Kong to the Japanese, he took his family to Makassar, Celebes, in the Dutch East Indies, to live with his wife's father. The father in law insisted that Young stay, too. There was no point in returning to Hong Kong, anyway. Nor could he avoid the Japanese much longer. They took the Dutch East Indies in March of 1942.

Jack Young's military career over the next two decades was Zeliglike. He'd risen to general's rank in the Chinese Army, in a unit that served as aides to Chiang Kaishek. But because he'd been born in Hawaii, he was drafted into the U.S. Army after the Japanese bombed Pearl Harbor in 1941. He stayed in China however, with a new U.S. Army rank of second lieutenant, which he later joked was "probably the biggest demotion in U.S. Army history."

In 1942, when General Joseph Stilwell was sent to China as an advisor to Generalissimo Chiang, Jack Young was an obvious choice as an aide. He knew Chiang and had worked directly for him—though that tidbit would not necessarily endear him to Stilwell. Stilwell and Chiang despised each other.

"He would see Jack Young as a spy for Chiang Kaishek in his operation," says Stephen MacKinnon, a history professor at Arizona State University who specializes in twentieth century Asian history. MacKinnon notes that Stilwell spoke Chinese and had lived in China. But Young claimed he asked for a transfer because he couldn't stand Stilwell's racism.

One day, in Young's presence, or so he told me, Stilwell muttered something to the effect of "These Chinamen can't do anything right," and when he realized Young was there, he quickly said, "Oh, but you're different."

"No I'm not," Young retorted. "I just speak English."

Young became an intelligence officer behind enemy lines, at times staying with his uncle in Shanghai, whose auto dealership had been confiscated by the Japanese. Young's main responsibility was to enlist farmers to search for American fliers shot down over China, and to establish safe houses for them until they could smuggle them back to safety. He was awarded his first Legion of Merit for that service.

Then, at war's end, President Harry Truman sent the newly retired general (and future Secretary of State) George Marshall to China to try to mediate between Chiang and the Communists. Jack Young was Marshall's aide and interpreter for the six months he was there, sleeping on a cot blocking Marshall's door for extra security. As interpreter, he sat in on Marshall's conferences with Chiang in Nanjiang ("Don't tell me anything you don't want me to pass on to the Americans, which is my country," he claims he said to Chiang) and with Mao Zedong and Zhou Enlai in the caves of Yenan.

"Mao is an introvert," Young told me. "If you know him well [and he was implying he did], after a few glasses of Chinese wine, he talks more openly."

Then he inadvertently slipped into Johnny Cochran-like doggerel: "Zhou Enlai, you don't have to pry. Without Zhou, there is no Mao."

He kept his ties on both sides. He had befriended a Peoples Army general named Ye Jian Ying. General Ye's daughter, a college student, was captured by Chiang's police, and so Ye asked Young for help. Young intervened with Marshall and an American plane was sent for the girl and spirited her away.

Later, when Young needed a return favor for his own family matters, there was none.

"You want to see a Japanese?" Quentin Young said to me one afternoon when he was in a playful mood. He took his wife, Swan's scarf from the back of a couch in his living room and draped it over the back of his head, then pulled on his brown baseball cap to anchor the scarf. It looked as if he were wearing a military cap with a bill on one side and a sun flap on the other. Then he stood up and strutted arrogantly around the living room while his wife laughed wickedly. They'd both lived through the Japanese occupation of the Dutch East Indies—though they didn't know each other until years later—and their resentment had hardly softened, even after 50 years.

The Indonesians welcomed the Japanese as liberators. And the Indonesian people have always disliked the Chinese. So after the Japanese took Makassar, Quentin Young had tried to fade into the background, but one of his wife Diana's friends, turned him in and told the Japanese about Young's close ties to the Chinese government. He was arrested and thrown in a detention camp. His father-in-law bailed him out a week later. But as part of his punishment, Young was forced to learn Japanese and undergo military training and then to teach military exercises to other Indonesians.

After sundown he did what he could to fight back. Every night in good weather, American and Australian planes would bomb the island. Reconnaissance planes would drop leaflets warning the islanders to evacuate, but since Young was a teacher, the Japanese soldiers would not allow him to leave town. So he dug a bomb shelter in his back yard.

One night the bombs walked down the street, and the last one flattened the house next door, while Young and his family trembled in the shelter, with dust filling their nostrils, the noise of the bombardment and the screams of the neighbors in their ears. Subsequently, he'd sneak his family out to the country after dark and bring them home after the planes had gone.

He claims he resisted in other ways. Following instructions on leaflets, he'd help lay out paper and cloth arrows to point out the locations of the Japanese ack-ack guns for attacking Allied planes. He would smuggle food to Australian prisoners of war, whom the Japanese forced to perform menial labor.

"They were trying to demoralize the Indonesians by saying, 'We caught these White people, and now they're cleaning streets,'" Young told me.

Or more likely they were trying to demoralize the Chinese and impress the Indonesians. But Young would leave food and cigarettes in the garbage cans so the prisoners would find them when they cleaned the cans.

The Japanese withdrew from the East Indies in the summer of 1945. Young helped Australian soldiers with mop-up maneuvers. There's a photograph in his picture albums of Young with two Australian soldiers. He's still young-looking, but the stress of the war is etched in lines on his handsome face. He's holding a rifle and posing over the carcass of a water buffalo they'd bagged. Young claimed that they were really hunting Japanese stragglers.

His second child, Charles, was born in the middle of it all in 1945. Young had torn feelings about what he would do next. He thought he'd return to China, but the Chinese consul, just released from an internment camp himself, asked Young to stay and work at the consulate, where he became head of the investigative section of the Overseas Chinese Association and passport officer for Makassar.

At the end of the war, the Allies handed the East Indies back to the Dutch, which touched off a fight for Indonesian independence led by Sukarno. Young's home faced the Celebes Sea, and he could watch the battleships offshore lobbing shells at inland targets. He remembers seeing Diana and his children hiding under the kitchen table as Indonesian troops came house to house down the street. Once an Indonesian soldier came to the door and claimed he'd left his Rolex watch on the window sill but now it was gone. Young took off his own watch and gave it to him so that he would go away.

In 1949, Sukarno allied himself with the Indonesian Communist party and broke off relations with Nationalist China—newly in exile on Taiwan—in favor of the People's Republic of China. As a Nationalist Chinese, Young was declared stateless, and his consulate job was rendered meaningless.

He refused to say exactly what he did for the next several years other than that he was a traveling merchant. Of what, there's no telling. He and Jack, whose lives were once so closely bound, now set out on different courses. Jack pressed straight ahead; Quentin was adrift again.

Ruth Harkness was wandering, too, trying hard to ignore the growing war while following her new metier as world traveler and author. But time was running out for her genre of travel writing. Too many Americans were about to be sent to places that were far more exotic than they wished to visit.

She had obviously written *The Lady and the Panda* before she returned to China on her second panda-hunting mission in 1937. It came out in 1938. She wrote a children's book about the same trip, and also before she returned to China, she pitched a book proposal about a chimpanzee she'd met and found clever enough, as she inadvertently put it, to seem interested in what she had to say.

Life at home was less than she desired, and the only thing she had to show for her new notoriety was a lawsuit filed by a seamstress who slipped and fell on an icy sidewalk outside her sister's home in Queens, where she lived some of the time. The woman sued Harkness for $50,000, thinking that Harkness had to be rich because of her books and her inheritance and her many trips to China.

In February of 1940, Harkness set sail again, this time for Peru, where, according to the *New York Times*, she would "study the descendants of the Incas for comparison to the inhabitants of Tibet." Harkness felt sure that since those peoples looked alike, they were probably related. Why she should be the one to make such a study is anyone's guess.

On the bio she typed out for her agent, she more cynically said that she and her cat were going to South America "because Jane Hardy (literary agent) said she couldn't read the stuff they had been writing and why didn't she go to Peru and write a book?"

So she did. This extended trip became another search for a rare and elusive animal. In the bio, Harkness just calls it a "mythic animal," but by the time the book came out it had become a silver bear that had only been seen once, and Harkness was just the person to prove that it existed. As a character in the next book said to her, "I am sure that you will find it, and that people all over the world will love it just as they have loved your baby pandas and in a way it will be a gift from Peru to the children of America."

Perhaps it was a transparent pretense, but nonetheless she moved from Lima to a village with a made-up name on the *ceja de selva*, the "eyebrow of the jungle," that place where the rain forest lurches up into the Andes. She had a native guide named Sandoval, with whom she held long, philosophical conversations.

The book was titled *Pangoan Diary*, and it came out in 1942. The *Saturday Review* called it "a most entertaining escape into a land where the people have never heard of today's catastrophic war." In the photo that accompanied the book review, Harkness wore an even more elaborate turban than usual.

It's hard to tell exactly what the book is about. It's not journalism. It's not really travelogue. It might be allegory. Mostly it's about Harkness's ability to withstand personal hardship while communing with native folk, for surely, as the book review points out, "She plunges into the hardships of native life wholehearted-ly, accepting whatever happens as part of the pattern of life."

But the pretense of the silver bear was vague and not very believable.

"I think a lot of that is really fiction," said her niece, Jane Jones. "To make things fit what her conception was, she was not beyond embroidering. She wanted to believe the tales the natives told her because she was a romantic."

When I asked if the same could be true of *The Lady and the Panda*, Jones replied, "It never occurred to us that she would misrepresent *that*. That would be criminal."

Harkness's stay in Peru was cut short when she came down with malaria.

"They hauled her out of the woods with a temperature of 105," said her sister, Harriet Anderson. "For a long time she couldn't do much."

Harkness described it thus: "Almost a year of primitive liv-ing produced various varieties of fever and infections which necessitated two months of operations, etc., etc., in the Clinica Americana in Lima."

And in a later magazine piece she vividly described what it's like to have malaria: "... with that strange phenomenon which is malarial fever, the cold of death settles in the bones, and no tropic sun can bring warmth until the chills pass.

"They last about an hour; there follows the reaction of vio-lent perspiration, then mercifully one can sleep. Not the least strange part of it is that one often feels rather well on waking, well enough to keep a dinner engagement."

She never shook the effects of the disease. Undaunted, she went to live in Mexico to try to sell yet another book about living alone in an exotic locale. As she put it, "I dislike the tyranny of possessions, preferring a mobile sort of existence."

She never sold the book. Instead, the Mexican stay was turned into a series of articles for *Gourmet* magazine under the running heading "Mexican Mornings." As a series, it touched on Harkness's usual themes: the nearly human wisdom of animals; the nobility of native peoples; and how Indians were really Orientals. And because she was writing for *Gourmet*, she worked the occasional recipe into the prose, as when she discovers an exotic delight they called "guacamole."

After Mexico, Harkness moved to Santa Fe, New Mexico. Jane Jones tried to visit her there when she was released from military service, but her aunt had already moved on to Taos.

Jones told me that she didn't like to talk about the last year of Ruth Harkness's life, preferring to keep it a family matter. Then, on further questioning, she admitted that Harkness drank heavily, and it may have been exacerbated by the lasting effects of malaria.

"We figured that maybe the illness [from Peru] affected her liver," Harriet Anderson concurred, "but she didn't take care of her health too well."

In 1946, Harkness reached back to her stay in Pangoa for more articles in *Gourmet,* and apparently that inspired her to go back to Peru to take another look around for the "silver bear." In late July of 1947, she traveled to Pittsburgh to meet with people who might possibly fund that voyage for her, and she checked into a room on the third floor of the Greer Hotel.

On Sunday, July 20, hotel employees opened her door after noticing that she hadn't come out of the room for some time. They found Harkness dead in a partly-filled bathtub. She'd been dead for hours.

Her *New York Times* obituary politely listed the cause of death as acute gastroenteritis, but *Time* magazine stated it more bluntly as acute alcoholism. She was just 46 years old, but she'd lived fast and hard, and proven she could do what the Great White Hunters could not.

When Harkness's sister Harriet died in 1997, the family finally marked Ruth's grave back home in Titusville, Pennsylvania, in a way she deserved, as "The Panda Lady Ruth McCombs Harkness."

CHAPTER THIRTEEN

YIN AND YANG

So much happened to the Young brothers in the chaos of Asia after the Second World War, most of it undocumented. The strongest memories of any life harken back to youth and early adulthood; then during middle-age, events seem to rocket by too quickly to register until suddenly, you're catapulted into old age without understanding exactly how you got there. So it is with the Young brothers' story.

Besides, these men were spies, and this account depends not only on their fading memories, but on their conflicting and unconfirmable stories as well. They were forever secretive, glossing over details as they edited their words, mistrusting even each other, and I was never certain at what point the embellishments, if any, became indistinguishable from the truth—even in their own minds.

"The truth is the truth," Quentin Young had told me, but what is truth? And whose truth are we talking about anyway? Jack and Quentin Young seemed to have different ideas about that. Throughout their lifetimes, Quentin resented Jack's authority and his ability to thrive in any circumstance; Jack resented Quentin's resentment. They were Yin and Yang: Jack, smiling and adventurous, always coming out on top; Quentin, melancholy, a black hole of misfortune, sucking bad luck into the void from every corner of the universe.

And perhaps they were deliberately vague because they weren't proud of everything they did. Su Lin Young told me that she remained in China with her husband Jack until 1943, but she evaded the question of when they actually split up. During the late 1940s, Jack fathered a child out of wedlock in Hong Kong. After Jack died, his second wife, June, still held a grudge agasinst Quentin for what she saw as disrespect for his older brother.

Quentin Young would only tell me that he had been a merchant traveling between Hong Kong and Indonesia from 1949 to 1953. In 1982, he wrote down his life story for a Jehovah's Witness magazine, fast-forwarding over the details, providing a short and sanitized summary for a painful period of his life.

"After the Japanese surrender, I reorganize the Overseas-Chinese in Indonesia and work in the Chinese consulate," he wrote. "But when Indonesia recognizes Communist China in 1949, we have to close down the consulate. I join the Nationalist Party and lead an Overseas-Chinese branch there and keep them loyal to Nationalist China. Because of this service, I am called back to the party headquarters in 1953, now in Taiwan. I am given special academic training, sent back to Indonesia, end up in jail once more in 1958 during their leftist regime."

Jack Young's U.S. Army career followed a trajectory as fast and true as a bullet's. He commanded an unconventional warfare unit in Korea during the Korean War, a unit made up of Army

Rangers, South Korean Army regulars and turncoat North Koreans. Officially he headed a security task force and oversaw South Korean police forces in his region. The unit provided intelligence and also helped evacuate refugees. His main purpose, as he explained it to me, was to turn Communist soldiers against their own armies, even if that was outside the accepted bounds of international law.

He apparently cut a large enough figure to get noticed by officials in the Peoples Republic of China. His parents were arrested at their ancestral home in Cui Heng. The news of their arrest was put out over radio broadcasts as a message for Jack Young. Young did not hear the broadcasts, and instead was told of them by a friend who worked in a radio intercept unit.

The message, as he summarized it to me was "If you want to come over to us, we'll release them."

Young had no intention of defecting, but he had an alternate plan, unauthorized, to exchange two of his Communist prisoners for his parents.

"I had lots of prisoners I didn't even turn in," he told me with a casual wave of the hand. "Don't forget: I am an unconventional force, not bound by rules."

He had a go-between in Hong Kong through whom he communicated to the Communists, and he set out for Hong Kong to try to complete the deal.

He also appealed to General Ye of the Peoples Army, whose daughter he had saved by intervening with U.S. Army General George Marshall a few years earlier. Ye would not reciprocate.

When Young reached Hong Kong, he found that his father had already been starved to death in prison. His mother was under house arrest. Years later he obtained her last letter, which he kept framed on the wall of his study, its neat rows of Chinese characters in marked contrast to the sloppy brush strokes of a letter from Chairman Mao that hung on a wall across the room.

He gave me a translation of his mother's heartbreaking letter:

"My third son Jack, I have the unmistakable premonition as if Buddha was speaking to me, that the village party cadre and Red Guards will return again to take me away as they did a few weeks ago to your father. When they came looking for him, your father was hiding in the attic behind the trap door double wall built in the days when the ocean pirates frequently raided us. When they were unable to locate him, they knocked me down, dragged me by the hair and beat me. Your father emerged from the hiding place to surrender when he no longer could stand my moaning from the beating being administered. He was then taken away with a rope around his neck to the county jail.

"I know you will be back one day as I have complete faith in Buddha who will protect you from harm and danger. This letter will be left with my dearest friend and nextdoor neighbor Widow Feng. You must see and talk to her. She has the details of what has happened to us. Help her too and take care of your brothers and sisters.

"Your Mother's last command, written under the light of the candle."

She died without ever leaving the house again, and despite her faith in Jack and Buddha, neither could rescue her.

Quentin Young was devastated when he learned of his parents' death, and his son, Charles told me that he wept for two days.

He also became virulently anti-Communist, and reported to Taiwan for the special training he referred to in his Jehovah's

Witness article. There's a photograph of Quentin and Jack Young together in Taiwan in 1953. Jack was there as a military advisor to Chiang Kaishek. He appears in uniform in the photo; Quentin is smartly turned out in a sport coat and slacks. Appropriately, they're sitting on opposite sides of a seesaw in a children's playground, a fitting metaphor for their relationship. It was the first time they'd seen each other since the late 1930s.

Quentin claimed he became a spy for Chiang Kaishek's Kuomintang party at that point. The Taiwan training, he said cynically, was a brainwashing of sorts, and he recalled how he and a table full of middle-aged men would sit, like youngsters at a military school, and wait for the Generalissimo and his wife to enter the dining hall, waiting until the Chiangs were seated and a general gave them permission to eat. As proof, Quentin would point to Chinese characters in long documents he said were Kuomintang records. I had no way of knowing if they really were or not.

Jack Young would change the subject when I asked about his brother's Kuomintang service. June Young, Jack's second wife, would guffaw outright. She was not unschooled in such matters: she had spent her life as a civilian employee of the U.S. Army, and when she and Jack met in 1954, she was a psychological warfare expert working at the Pentagon. She claimed that Quentin was spying not for the Kuomintang, but for anti-Communist forces in Indonesia. Ultimately, it might have amounted to the same thing. And Quentin Young would have been performing that duty not out of love for Nationalist China so much as hatred for the ideologues who killed his parents.

But he returned to Indonesia as editor of a Chinese-language newspaper in Surabaya, which gave him reason to travel extensively and to have a reporter's access to Sukarno's palace, where he says he befriended some of the guards. His album bears photos of himself carrying an old-fashioned newsman's camera with a chrome flash.

In 1955 he changed jobs—or "covers," as he put it—and became the assistant manager of a bank. It was there, in 1958, that his undercover activities were exposed to the authorities. There was a cell of spies at the bank. The director and another assistant manager were first identified as foreign agents and arrested. The director bribed his way out of trouble, according to Young, and the other assistant manager disappeared, though Young never made clear if the latter fled or was imprisoned. The manager's wife fingered Young, asking police why he hadn't been arrested, too, since he was in the thick of it with her husband. When the police came to call on Young, they learned of his past association with the Nationalist Chinese consulate. They figured out who Jack was, and they hauled Quentin off to prison.

"They welcomed me," as Young put it, his voice dropping into its least audible registers.

They isolated him in a pitch black cell, beat him, burned him with cigarettes and a cattle prod.

"At first it was painful—a shock and you feel burning, then later I just lay there and I didn't care. I didn't feel it anymore."

So his torturers changed tactics. They became soft, imploring. Why couldn't he just cooperate?

"They put a light bulb in my face and they asked me a lot of questions," Young said, "and I told them, 'Well, you can just consider me as dead. What can I say? If I say 'no,' you say 'yes.' I have told you everything already.'

"This was continuous, day in and day out, for many, many days. Every time they came to see me I'd say, 'Go do your duty, yeah? If you were me, would you tell people you were a subversive, a spy? You know already. It's no use to keep me here. I won't tell you anything.'"

When they gave him rotten food crawling with insects, he gave up completely, refused to eat, and decided to die. His wife Diana could not find anyone to help locate him. The family friends were worried that if they came to her assistance, they'd only be marked for trouble with the government themselves. But she did track him down, brought him food, brought his adolescent children to visit. Young told them, "You can consider me gone."

After six months, Young's health deteriorated so badly that the authorities worried he'd die in prison, and so they sent him home under house arrest. He recovered physically before he recovered emotionally.

"I was kind of crazy for a while," he said without elaborating further.

He carried the physical and the emotional scars for the rest of his life. In fact, it took several sessions to get him to talk about it, and whenever he did, he would invariably stay awake all night, alone with his terrifying memories and then cancel our meetings for the next day so that he could recuperate from the psychic discomfort.

In the years after his imprisonment, he went from house arrest to city arrest to state arrest. And even after he returned to his job at the bank, police officers would show up to lean on him, press him for information, and he claimed he would feed them misinformation, and then live in fear of being sent back to prison.

In 1960, Diana took ill with cancer and died. She was 44; Young was 46. In the photographs taken at the time of the funeral, his hair is still jet black, almost as black as the look on his face. He grieved for the rest of his life. Even 30 years into his second marriage he still spoke of Diana as "The Girl in the Red Sweater."

Six years later he met Swan, an assistant manager at the bank. She was an ethnic Chinese from Borneo, but even though her family had been in Indonesia for three generations, she was not considered Indonesian because of the anti-Chinese sentiment that has always existed in that country. She didn't even speak Chinese, and since Young spoke very little Indonesian, they communicated in English, which she had learned in school. They married a year later.

Sukarno was overthrown in a coup in 1966, and so Quentin had less to fear politically. In 1968, he and Swan immigrated to Taiwan. Young's children were already adults. They waited until Charles's first child was born, held her in their arms, and then left the country.

They'd obtained tourist visas, with no intent of returning. Jack claimed that he pulled strings with the Taiwanese government to make it happen—a statement that made Quentin bluster, however likely it was.

As they boarded a plane, a customs officer confiscated their money, saying she'd hold it for them until they came back. After all, they wouldn't be able to spend it in Taiwan.

"Perhaps it's best you don't come back," the officer then said to Swan.

"Why not?" she asked.

"You're just eating up all our rice."

* * *

Jack Young went from posts in Taiwan to Vietnam, where he served on the Joint Intelligence Staff under General William Westmoreland, who was then the commander of US Forces in Vietnam. And true to form, he wouldn't say exactly what he did there, other than say that he continued to go behind enemy lines as he had done in Korea and World War II.

"It was easy for me to infiltrate," he told me. "Same as in Korea. My problem was getting out. I had to cross American lines, and I had a hell of a time convincing them that I am no gook."

He never thought of any other career.

"What would I be? A bank manager?" he once said to me, perhaps taking an intentional dig at his brother's many derailed careers. He had married a military woman and led a military life.

"You crave the excitement, so I never complained," he told me. "Uncle Sam has been good to me. I am glad to be alive. I have no complaints about Agent Orange or GI benefits. I am goddamned glad to be alive!"

But he was passed over for promotion. He'd reached the rank of full colonel, but the general's star had evaded him. Quentin thought it was because of the illegitimate son he'd fathered. Nonetheless Jack was thinking of postponing retirement and doing another tour of duty in Vietnam to see if he could finally get the promotion.

"You are getting old," Quentin claims he told Jack, in a rare case of the younger brother dispensing advice to the older brother. "Is it worth it if all that returns with a general's rank is your name?"

Jack Young did his last tour of duty in Missouri and retired in 1968 after 24 years in the U.S. Army. He'd been awarded two Silver Stars, three Bronze Stars, and two Legions of Merit from the Army, and the Order of Yun Hui from the Chinese government. He and June moved to suburban St. Louis, into the old white house with the carved Chinese furniture in the living room, and the snow-leopard pelt over the back of a couch.

Quentin Young found peace and respectability in Taiwan.

"He was so full of hope when we lived there," says his wife Swan.

He'd tried at first to rejuvenate a failing government newspaper there. He organized a committee to try to reestablish trade relations with Indonesia. And he claims the Kuomintang ignored his assertions that he was due some sort of back pay for his service and imprisonment while in Indonesia. Still, he was full of hope. Then in 1969, he landed a job in the personnel department at RCA's Taiwan office, and he edited an in-house publication for the corporation.

In 1974, Jack was ill, and he asked Quentin to come live in the United States, as family should. Quentin claims he was just months away from being 60 years old and therefore eligible for pension, but he went out of loyalty to his brother. It added one more cause for resentment to the long list he'd been keeping.

Jack's version was that he had to pull strings to get Quentin out of Taiwan while he still had political strings to pull. Because Quentin did not have any birth records, it was impossible to show that he was the son of an American citizen. Jack's citizenship was not enough proof for the Immigration and Naturalization Service. Quentin had to go through the naturalization process as if he were just another foreigner.

Quentin was working in the sports department of a St. Louis K-mart when Hollywood called. While in Taiwan, he and Swan had become Jehovah's Witnesses, and they were approached by an American member of the congregation who thought he could land them a movie deal. The would-be producer bought Quentin's life story for a song and bought the rights to *The Lady and the Panda,* and then commissioned a screenplay with religious overtones.

Since Quentin had been unable to get along with Jack, anyway, in 1982, he moved to San Diego so that he could more easily collaborate with his Hollywood producers. His son, Charles, who had become a successful businessman in Indonesia, moved into a spacious house a few blocks away from his father's little apartment. His daughter, Jenny, was a few hours north in the San Francisco area.

For the next decade, Quentin and Jack seldom spoke to each other, though they did go to China together in 1984 to reclaim the family's ancestral home in Cui Heng. When they got there, to Quentin's perpetual dismay, there was a plaque on the wall proclaiming it the ancestral home of Colonel Jack T. Young. They seldom spoke after that.

The movie deal languished, then seemed to disappear altogether. In 1992, it suddenly reappeared when Young received a call from a new producer saying his associates had bought a contract that Young thought had expired. The project changed form a few more times, went into hibernation, and then, in 2000, the movie was finally made with little or no input from Young.

When it screened in the summer of 2001, Quentin and Swan Young attended the premiere in the company of their lawyers. Young was so bitter that he refused to attend any post-screening parties or speak to reporters.

Horseback adventurers. Courtesy Mrs. Vivian Dai.

CHAPTER FOURTEEN

INDIANA JONES
LIVES NEAR THE MALL

On a warm September morning, I drove to Balboa Park in San Diego to do some panda hunting of my own. I brought one of my daughters with me; she knew the story well, because when she was five years old, Swan and Quentin Young gave her a tiny panda charm. And as a kindergartner on class trips to the Field Museum in Chicago, she used to point out the stuffed remains of Su Lin to her classmates and teachers and say, "That's the panda that my father's friend brought from China." Now she was in college.

We circled the park for a parking space, and then, appropriately, found a ricksha (this one bicycle-powered) to take us to the zoo gates, where we plopped down $50 and ventured along sidewalks as crowded as any Chinese city street that had delighted Ruth Harkness.

There was abundant panda sign—signs I should say—arrows, in fact, that led us on a winding hike past cages and snack bars and gift shops. To stay in the mood, my daughter bought an outrageously tasteless soft drink cup that featured the head of a panda with a straw sticking out of its ear.

I had expected to waltz in and see a panda and then waltz out, but on that day, pandas in the zoo were as hard to find as pandas in the wild. To my surprise, there were at least 100 people waiting in line to get into the panda exhibit, many of them Chinese come to see a *xiongmao,* or "bear cat," as pandas are now called in China. We waited our turn, and when we finally reached the gate, a guard standing there was telling the crowd over and over that neither of the pandas were outside, but rather had gone into the air conditioned parts of their enclave where they were out of sight. We filed through anyway, peering at the transplanted bamboo trees, hoping for a glimpse. But there was none.

Right next to the panda exhibit, however, was a gift shop, several thousand square feet of panda paraphernalia: hats, t-shirts, pictures, and other bric-a-brac. The reason zoos fight so hard to get giant pandas is because despite the fact that they don't do much other than eat and sleep, they are incredibly prolific money makers.

I don't even remember the pandas' names. I think they were called "No Sho" and "Cha-Ching." And if not, they should have been.

Halfway back across Balboa Park, a theater in the park's science center was screening the movie, purportedly based on the true story of Ruth Harkness and her baby panda. I had seen early scripts of the proposed film project, and they stayed fairly close to history. Oh sure, there were some Hollywood flourishes: in an early scene, Ruth seeks out a Russian woman in Shanghai who was allegedly Bill Harkness's girlfriend. As best as I could figure, the allusion came from Jack Young's speculation about Bill in a letter to the curators at the American Museum of Natural

History. And in the tradition of Hollywood adventure, there were the expected stunts with collapsing bridges and crack shots.

The finished film, however, was pure fiction: they'd gutted the true story and replaced it with one they made up. This Ruth Harkness was drop-dead gorgeous, and its Quentin, though quite handsome, was no idealistic young hero, no adventure-some modern man, but rather a smiling and obsequious Oriental lackey.

In this version of the "true" story, Bill Harkness was a biologist observing pandas in the wild when he died of a mysterious fever. The real Bill Harkness never got within a hundred miles of a panda, and the study of animals in their habitat was decades away. This Quentin Young had been one of Bill Harkness's intrepid companions on the expedition. The real Quentin Young never even met the man. And in the movie there is an evil big game hunter whose name is neither Smith nor Jones, but Johnston, and he engages the heroes in a race to get to Bill Harkness's pandas.

Of course, the real Ruth Harkness never saw a panda in the wild other than the one she and Young found in the hollow tree. But in the movie she watches three over the course of several scenes, and when the evil hunter kills two, she rescues the third, a cub, and brings it home to civilization. Right before the credits run, a voiceover announces that the made-up hunter, Johnston, never shot a panda again. I suppose he didn't, because he didn't exist.

Meanwhile, the real Quentin Young was living in a barely affordable three-room apartment in a beach town 30 miles to the north of Balboa Park. His wife, Swan, was well past retirement age, but she still worked at a local bank to earn enough money to make ends meet. Despite the dollars generated by pandas down in Balboa Park—indeed by his own story—they'd struggled financially.

For as long as I've known him, Quentin's health has been failing slowly and steadily. He's had strokes and gout. His eyesight and hearing have deteriorated, as if he is dying by degrees.

In the spring of 2001, he called me out of the blue. His voice was slurred, and I could tell he'd suffered another stroke, and it seemed to affect his personality. He struggled through a few questions and then grew unexplainably angry. It was the last I ever spoke to him.

When we first met during the late 1980s, Swan would drive us around town in her little car, screeching and swerving like any California driver, while Quentin pointed out the sites, which in that part of the world consisted mostly of chain restaurants and shopping malls, a far cry from Tibetan peaks and Sichuanese bamboo thickets.

Back then, I had some trouble reconciling the old man in the front seat of the car with the handsome and fearless young man of his photo album. How could it be that Indiana Jones now lived near the mall? Or for that matter, in suburban St. Louis? Jack Young, by comparison to his brother, had seemed tireless and timeless. I could still hear danger in his crackling voice, see the cunning in his icy eyes. Talking to either one of them was always a bit like a chess match, and they were better players than I.

Quentin's photo album highlights what a remarkable time and place he and Jack lived in during the first half of the twentieth century. The native peoples standing next to the modern young men in the pictures might just as well have stepped out of a time machine, if they came from the same planet at all. The distances the brothers traveled every time they ventured into that past weren't much greater, say, than traveling from New York to Chicago, distances that, today, could be covered in a matter of hours. But back then they might as well have been light years.

It took me nearly a decade to merge the face of the fearless young man in the photographs onto the body of the old man in the front seat of Swan's car, but eventually I did. Quentin Young was still bright and inquisitive. He could pull random facts out of the air: elevations of mountains, names of politicians. While his eyesight held up, he read voraciously, and that kept him attuned to the world outside his double-locked apartment door. He was still stunningly idealistic despite his great bitterness. At his most difficult, he was still admirable. The young man and the old man were one and the same, whether or not they lived near the mall.

In the purportedly true movie story, the Ruth and Bill Harkness characters (sanitized for our protection) were out to prove that pandas were wonderful creatures. Indeed they are. But I somehow find it more interesting that the real Bill Harkness—indeed all the Great White Hunters—didn't know a damned thing about giant pandas, and wanted to pursue them anyway, just because.

The Hollywood Harknesses are perfect. The real ones were tragically flawed, and yet far more interesting than the movie's cardboard cut outs. Ruth was insecure, headstrong, amoral, and all of those seemingly bad qualities drove her to pull off the kind of adventure that is almost too perfect for the movies. To my mind, she is all the more worthy of our respect.

More than one writer and more than one movie star has looked at Ruth Harkness's story as a "vehicle," as a saga of feminism. They base that impression on the strength of Harkness's

Jack Young in his later years.
Courtesy June Young.

somewhat embellished first book and her first adventure, and probably on their own hopes and dreams or lack thereof.

And the Chinese man? Once again, he's conveniently forgotten. It ruins the story for him to know more than the heroine. Jack Young pushed his younger brother to help this determined but naive American woman. Quentin Young made Harkness's adventure possible, provided the direction and the passion she needed, and got Harkness through insurmountable odds. She was grateful to him for that, even if no one heard her say so numerous times. Quentin Young is the crucial element that her later adventures and her later books lacked. The truth is slippery enough while the informants are still living.

Jack Young died on October 7, 2000, at the age of 89. Despite his earlier claims to me that he had not been sickened by Agent Orange while in Vietnam, his widow June thinks it contributed to his eventual affliction with non-Hodgkin's lymphoma. He was buried in Arlington National Cemetery.

Quentin Young is the last specimen of an endangered species: the early twentieth century explorer-adventurer-naturalist—the very words are useless and outdated in today's world. Jack Young was the next to last.

The animal they hunted is the archetypal endangered species. Cute and cuddly, the giant panda became the emblem of a major environmental organization. Giant pandas still draw crowds to zoos, just as they did in 1937, when Harkness brought hers to Chicago. Zookeepers and politicians alike are more than happy to find ways to skirt environmental laws in order to bring the beasts into the country. In the mid-1980s, the Chinese government discovered that pandas were not only goodwill ambassadors, but cash cows as well.

As panda expert George Schaller told me years ago, "Pandas don't bring out the best in people. There's money involved, and greed shows up."

We, the public continue to love them to death, though their plight in the wild is improving. There are now 33 panda preserves in China covering over 50 percent of their natural range. The Chinese government has made great strides to curtail poaching and restrict logging. Schaller tells me that the numbers are increasing, though he could not divulge the preliminary results of the panda census that was underway at this writing.

But this is not a book about pandas, it's about the panda hunters. They didn't care about the environment or about the animals' welfare. They cared about who would be the first to bring one out of the wild—a race that seems silly today in light of the animal's precarious existence. But at the time it seemed worthy enough to risk a life.

Quentin Young has an apartment full of pandas: panda books, panda pictures, panda trinkets hung on walls and stacked on shelves. "Not one of these did I buy," he once said to me, his voice rising to a crescendo. They were showered on him by friends and relatives with the best intentions. He claimed that he really hated pandas. He thought them evil. They just act like clowns to get people to feed them, he said. They hide their true intent with those big black patches around the eyes. He said it over and over.

Some day there may not be any more pandas left to hunt. But by then, the panda hunters will have long been extinct.

ACKNOWLEDGMENTS

This book was researched and written in two stages that were more than ten years apart, starting with a pair of magazine articles published in *International Wildlife* and the *San Diego Reader*. Much of it is based on interviews I conducted in the late 1980s and early 1990s with eyewitnesses—Jack and Quentin and Su Lin Young, Ruth Harkness's surviving relatives, and others, many of whom had passed away by the time I finished writing—and on documents I culled from the archives of the Field Museum in Chicago, the American Museum of Natural History in New York, and other institutions. And though I put the book aside for more than ten years, I kept in regular contact with Quentin Young, talking to him frequently on the telephone and visiting him whenever I was in San Diego. Since Jack Young's death, I've had conversations as well with his daughter Jolly Young and his second wife, June Young.

I relied on a number of helpful texts from the period, especially Ruth Harkness's books, *The Lady and the Panda* (1938) and to a lesser extent, *Pangoan Diary* (1942). *Men Against the Clouds,* by Richard L. Burdsall and Arthur B. Emmons, 3rd, with contri-

*Michael Kiefer at the Field Museum with the remains of Su Lin.
Courtesy John Murphy.*

butions by Terris Moore and Jack Theodore Young, which was first published in 1935 and then reissued in 1980 by The Mountaineers, details the first ascent of Minya Konka. I also made good use of Theodore and Kermit Roosevelt's *Trailing the Giant Panda* (1929) and Hassoldt Davis's *Land of the Eye* (1941). And I came across a cache of *China Journal* issues in the library at Arizona State University, which were helpful in corroborating the stories I'd already heard from the Young brothers. Staffers at *Gourmet* magazine dug some of Ruth Harkness's articles out of their files for me; I was delighted in 2001, when that magazine reprinted a piece about her winter in Zhaopo.

I'd like to express my great thanks to Jon Fisher at *International Wildlife* magazine for first calling Ruth Harkness to my attention. George Schaller, Chris Catton and Vicki Croke generously shared valuable information and were supportive of the project over the years.

Barry Graham and Kate Nolan helped me put the proposal in order.

John Murphy, Susannah Blackmon, and Adriana Mena gave crucial production support. Stephen MacKinnon of Arizona State University read the manuscript for historical accuracy, George Schaller for zoological accuracy (and because he's always liked the story). June Young and Mary Lobisco provided photographs. Hank Tusinski painted the panda frontispiece.

Thank you, John Oakes.

And of course, again, thank you, Quentin Young.

Buddha at Kiating. Courtesy Mrs. Vivian Dai.

INDEX